Frances Cleveland
1864 - 1947

Edith Roosevelt
1861 - 1948

Helen Taft
1861 - 1943

Ellen Wilson
1860 - 1914

Edith Wilson
1872 - 1961

Florence Harding
1860 - 1924

Grace Coolidge
1879 - 1957

Lou Hoover

Bess Trumam
1885 - 1982

Mamie Eisenhower
1896 - 1979

Pat Nixon
1912 - 1993

Betty Ford
1918 -

Barbara Bush
1925 -

Heart and Soul of the Nation

How The Spirituality Of Our First Ladies Changed America

PUBLISHED BY DOUBLEDAY
a division of Bantam Doubleday Dell Publishing Group, Inc.
1540 Broadway, New York, New York 10036

DOUBLEDAY and the portrayal of an anchor with a dolphin are trademarks of Doubleday, a division of Bantam Doubleday Dell Publishing Group, Inc.

BOOK DESIGN BY DANA LEIGH TREGLIA

Library of Congress Cataloging-in-Publication Data
Heckler-Feltz, Cheryl.
Heart and soul of the nation: how the spirituality of our first ladies changed America / Cheryl Heckler-Feltz. — 1st ed.
p. cm.
Includes bibliographical references.
1. Presidents' spouses—United States—Religious life.
2. Presidents' spouses—United States—Biography. I. Title.
E176.2.H44 1997
973'.099—dc20 96-43651
CIP

ISBN 0-385-48519-0

Printed in the United States of America
January 1997

1 3 5 7 9 10 8 6 4 2

First Edition

In honor of my mother and grandmother,
who sparked my interest in the First Ladies
and in honor of the women of Susannah Circle
who cheered my efforts,
I especially dedicate this book to my daughter, Leah,
and her generation of women who will carry forward
the legacy of the Beatitudes.

Acknowledgments

Researching and writing this text was a great journey, and I am especially grateful to the following:

To Mark Fretz at Doubleday for his enthusiasm for this subject and his support in seeing it through to completion.

To my husband, Glenn, and our children, Brady and Leah, for their continued support in all my professional endeavors, and to the extended Feltz and Heckler clans, who placed a blessing on my head when they claimed me as their own.

To my agent, Tom Thompson, as well as Sealy and Susan Yates, for their excellent professional assistance and teamwork. Tom especially recognized the potential of this project, and I credit him strongly for its success.

To Edith Mayo, curator of the political history division and First Ladies exhibit at the Smithsonian Institution, for her early support and encouragement.

To Patrick Vance, my editor at the *New York Times* Syndicate, as always, for his humor, grace, and professional skill.

To Jessica Wehrman, my research assistant, who, more than any other professional peer, has seen me at my very best and very worst. On this project we worked side by side at times, sorting through the stacks of books and files around us, our conversations almost always beginning, "Wow, listen to this."

To Dr. Donald Rogers, my mentor at United Theological Seminary, for teaching me which ones are the important voices and to Rev. Donald Hilkerbaumer, who is my spiritual director and a true Benedictine at heart.

To the staff of the Champaign County Library, who prove that behind every serious author is a group of hardworking librarians willing to tolerate the most obscure requests. To Grant and Demora Holcomb at TeaBaggers, where I read most of those library books.

To my closest friends—applause here—Janet, Peg, Marvy, and The Very Proper Miss Jill. Loyalty is a tremendous gift.

Contents

The Beatitudes

Blessed are the poor in spirit, for theirs is the kingdom of heaven.

Blessed are those who mourn, for they will be comforted.

Blessed are the meek, for they will inherit the earth.

Blessed are those who hunger and thirst
for righteousness, for they will be filled.

Blessed are the merciful,
for they will be shown mercy.

Blessed are the pure in heart,
for they will see God.

Blessed are the peacemakers,
for they will be called sons of God.

Blessed are those who are persecuted
because of righteousness, for theirs is the
kingdom of heaven.

*Blessed are you when people insult you,
persecute you and falsely say all kinds of evil
against you because of me. Rejoice and be glad,
because great is your reward in heaven, for in the
same way they persecuted the prophets
who were before you.*

—Matthew 5:3-12

Introduction

The Beatitudes are among the most cherished passages of the New Testament, a series of statements attributed to Jesus and recorded in the Gospel of St. Matthew 5:3–12 as part of Christ's Sermon on the Mount. (Luke records a similar series of sayings in 6:20–23.) This sermon is to the New Testament what the Ten Commandments are to Hebrew scripture—moral laws that establish a foundation considered essential to the spiritual development of an individual, a family, a community, even a nation. But unlike the Decalogue's famous "Thou shalt nots," Christ gave instruction on the subject of attitude and character, elements intended to lead to a lifestyle of self-evaluation and service to others, in addition to producing great personal joy, magnanimity, and good fortune.

At first Christ is speaking only in the presence of his specially selected disciples. This is a significant image because for one identified as a follower of the teachings of Christ, the Beatitudes offer spiritual insight that is as close to the nature of Jesus as the disciples were to his human form that day on the mountain. In other words, understanding the Beatitudes is essential to understanding the nature of Christ, and his followers should take note.

Sometime during the lesson a crowd gathers to hear Jesus, and by the end of his sermon he is teaching a multitude and so the lesson for disciples becomes more widely broadcast. This is an endearing, even prophetic bit of symbolism and foreshadowing, I think, because the beauty, poetry, and values of the Beatitudes makes them extremely attractive for those seeking wisdom in Judaism and Islam as well as people looking to Christianity but who do not consider themselves mainline moderates or conservative fundamentalists.

If traditional church teaching applies, we as individuals must first internalize and then continuously reexamine the Beatitudes as the circumstances of our lives evolve. Through this passage, Christ consoles his followers with short, emphatic benedictions pronounced over the actual, literal poverty and persecution they endure. These are, in fact, lessons regarding a blessed life, however ironic. "Blessed are the poor in spirit . . . those who mourn . . . the meek." Who among us, unless harboring a morbid obsession or total lack of self-preservation, would read farther? This all seems costly and absurd—an upside-down view of the world.

However, the last part of each Beatitude offers a more detailed description of a blessed life: "Theirs is the kingdom of heaven; they will be comforted; they will inherit the earth; they will be filled; they will be shown mercy; they will see God; they will be called sons of God."

Attributed to the Messiah and sifted through the intellectual and spiritual filter of the writer of Matthew's gospel, this concept of being blessed offers consolation following the inevitable difficulties of life. Jesus promises his disciples freedom to move about with a sense of heirship and security in God's world, and joy and fulfillment. There is grace and beauty, spiritual illumination, and, finally, full recognition as one of God's own.

Jesus's sermon was not a warning as much as specific encouragement to rise above what my grandmother called simply "the worldly world," to persevere in dedication to your spiritual journey, to claim a unique sense of freedom. The Beatitudes demonstrate that standard Christian dictum: The best way to find happiness is not to seek it directly. Instead, focus your aim toward holiness. The sweetest liberation, he is saying, is found in giving yourself without reserve to that lifestyle which you know in your heart to be right and true.

We can read the list—blessed are the peacemakers, the merciful, those who hunger and thirst for righteousness—and think of leaders in our own communities or states who have toughed it out as advocates for the less fortunate. We might even think of international leaders who shaped world events or claimed the Nobel Peace Prize. In American history, however, no group of individuals offers a better example of Christ's Beatitudes than our First Ladies.

"Blessed are the poor in spirit,
for theirs is the kingdom of God."

While the word "spirit" appears more than five hundred times throughout the Bible, "poor in spirit" appears only in this passage, and scholars typically offer three interpretations:

Those who are completely broken by life's events and simply not able to function within or contribute appropriately to their roles and personal circumstances. First Ladies Jane Pierce and Mary Lincoln are two examples of this.

Those who are determined to overcome their own obstacles and tragedies. Through this interpretation we find some of the most inspiring stories about our First Ladies, especially Betty Ford and Eleanor Roosevelt.

Those who observe brokenness and tragedy in the lives of others and respond with empathy and action. An elemental and consistent theme in the lives of our First Ladies, this point is interwoven with the concepts of righteousness and mercy as celebrated in the fourth and fifth Beatitudes.

"Blessed are those who mourn, for they will be comforted."

Like the first Beatitude, this is often interpreted at three levels: Those who are broken by loss; those who deliberately, determinedly reach past their own overwhelming grief to help others face a tragedy; and those who, in general, maintain an empathy and sensitivity to the common human experience of emotional suffering.

For all her achievements as First Lady—promoting the arts, winning the admiration of foreign leaders, restoring the White House—Jackie Kennedy's greatest gift to her country was her response to the assassination of her husband, John Kennedy. From the moment she stepped off the president's plane in her bloodstained suit at Andrews Air Force Base on the night of November 22, 1963, she led the nation through a three-day period of mourning with dignity, grace, and humility. Her exemplary behavior was so effective in its emotional and spiritual impact, young Jackie Kennedy—a thirty-four-year-old widow and mother of two—literally emerged as the most admired woman in the world.

"Blessed are the meek, for they will inherit the earth."

Meekness is a tired, discarded, misunderstood characteristic in America, typically confused with "weakness." Throughout the Bible, however, the word almost always is associated with strong characteristics such as godliness, temperance, self-discipline and applied wisdom. Martha Washington was meek. Abigail Adams wanted to be but believed she fell short of the goal too often.

"Blessed are those who hunger and thirst for righteousness, for they shall be filled."

This Beatitude reflects perhaps the greatest contribution our First Ladies have made to social reform in America. Throughout Hebrew scripture as well as the New Testament, righteousness is linked to personal action, integrity, and vigilance. This is not noblesse oblige, not just a nice thing to do if you find the time; rather, it reflects bulldog tenacity. One profound example is the day Lucy Hayes surprised White House visitors by announcing that she rebuked slavery with such thoroughness she wished she could have served President Lincoln with a garrison of women at Fort Sumter.

"Blessed are the merciful, for they will be shown mercy."

The fifth Beatitude is probably the easiest to define because of mercy's inevitable link to simplicity. Mercy doesn't ask a lot of questions, and it usually doesn't even ask "Does this person deserve assistance?" It simply acts—and, in so doing, is a faith statement that says even more about the giver than the receiver. Mercy is linked to justice, grace, and human dignity. It is a deliberate act that begins with empathy, develops as the giver concludes she can and must contribute *something* to the situation, and ends with the action itself. For First Ladies, it may be as easy as helping a stranger who sends a note to the White House for assistance or as dangerous as Pat Nixon's trip to Peru in 1970 after an earthquake killed more than 65,000 there.

The daughter of a Presbyterian minister, First Lady Ellen Wilson regularly visited Washington, D.C's poorest citizens, fed them, and promised to do what she could to improve their plight. Ellen's efforts were consistent and tireless: She lobbied Congress through her husband's office to improve housing; she gave tours of the slums to whoever had the stomach for the sight; and when she discovered she was dying, Ellen Wilson wondered, "Who will look after them when I am gone?"

"Blessed are the pure in heart, for they will see God."

Best translated "single-mindedness with your sights set on God," this admonishment—with its promise of spiritual illumination—has been fulfilled in the lives of many First Ladies. One of the most poignant examples is offered by Rosalynn Carter, who has worked for more than a quarter century to raise awareness and improve conditions for America's mentally ill and mentally retarded citizens, a cause created and developed directly from her spiritual beliefs.

"Blessed are the peacemakers,
for they will be called sons of God."

One of the strongest admonishments in scripture related to peace, this Beatitude promises that those who settle fights, those who promote the concept of universal justice and basic human rights are direct heirs of the Creator. In December 1945, President Harry Truman appointed Eleanor Roosevelt as a delegate to the newly formed United Nations organization, and as a member of the UN's Human Rights Commission she was a significant contributor in drafting a Universal Declaration of Human Rights and winning its acceptance by the General Assembly. This was just one of her many efforts toward domestic and international peace and justice.

"Blessed are you when people insult you and falsely say all kinds of evil against you because of me. Rejoice and be glad, because great is your reward in heaven, for in the same way the persecuted the profits who were before you."

Persecution steals life, and persecution in the name of any deity certainly is among the greatest evils related to our humanness. Persecution's greatest victim is human dignity, and America has not yet had—and likely never will have—a First Lady who escapes the overwhelming demoralizing, humiliating experience of reading stories about herself which are blatant, outright assaults on her character based on rumors, malicious intents, or political manipulation. Vitriolic attacks by the conservative religious right on Hillary Clinton have damaged her public image, but in 1828 those attacks cost Rachel Jackson her life.

"Rejoice and be glad, for your reward is great in heaven, for so they persecuted the prophets who were before you."

Jesus makes it clear in the Beatitudes that he is calling us to a lifestyle often in contrast to that of the wealthy and powerful. Likewise in our nation's history, First Ladies typically have served as the most capable guardians of the least among us. From Martha Washington's aid to the poorest soldiers at Valley Forge to Abigail Fillmore's work in education and literacy and Hillary Clinton's determination in child advocacy, our First Ladies' actions almost always are linked to their religious training. Often controversial, always criticized by somebody, these women can easily understand Christ's warning of persecution and appreciate his promise that "your reward is great in heaven . . ." because it's certainly a mixed bag in this lifetime.

The Gift of the First Ladies

Their spiritual contributions are profound and heartwarming. They created orphanages following war, immunized children, improved public education, started hospitals, established libraries, promoted church involvement, provided for the elderly, and even taught Sunday school. Our First Ladies have become America's conscience—the heart and soul of the nation.

While my own interest in the First Ladies began many years ago, it wasn't until after I completed a series of interviews and then brief personal conversations with Rosalynn Carter from 1992 through 1995 on the subject of spirituality that the idea for this text took shape. Mrs. Carter was the impetus for my decision to collect vignettes describing actions taken by all First Ladies as a result of their religious beliefs.

I read their journals and their letters, and I discovered many fascinating details: Martha Washington's daily prayer rituals; Lucretia Garfield's conclusion that women's suffrage was literally atheistic; Julia Gardiner Tyler's conversion to Catholicism toward the end of her life, and the Protestant social reform model that influenced most of these women. I even read one dusty text about Anna Symmes Harrison, wife of ninth president William Henry, which delighted me in its conclusion: "Her grandson, Benjamin Harrison, is the present Republican candidate for the Presidency." I transformed the information into a three-part series for the *New York Times* Syndicate and knew from the response it received that the time was right for a book as well.

Still, the framework for this text didn't surface until the day I began to reexamine—as part of my own devotional studies—the Beatitudes, and I realized I wasn't studying just Christ's admonishments. I was seeing the collective religious experience of our nation's First Ladies. I jumped up from my desk, certain a more appropriate outline was not possible. From there the book production began in earnest, and the text soon took on its own life-form.

If there is merit in this text, it will be found in the simplicity of the stories themselves. My task here is not to offer a deep theological analysis of their lives, for that would be encumbering and uninviting—perhaps even rigid and myopic. Rather, my job was to sift through the Beatitudes and First Ladies' stories simultaneously to see which gems surfaced. It was an engaging bit of work.

Martha Washington and Eleanor Roosevelt drew my admiration; Rosalynn Carter and Lucy Hayes, my affection; Betty Ford and Lady Bird Johnson, my determination to emulate their ability to balance grace with honesty. Florence Harding drew my pity and derision; Hillary Clinton, my absolute certainty that history will acknowledge her spirituality with greater clarity and appreciation than our current political and religious environment will allow.

Remarkably, there exists no published compilation of the religious lives and spiritual contributions of our nation's First Ladies, though as a nation we tend to cherish these women and their "kinder, gentler" contributions to the ugly, brutal game of presidential politics.

The Soul of the Nation

Of the forty-five women whom historians identify as presidential wives, more than thirty are associated with the Episcopal, Methodist, Presbyterian, or Baptist denominations. Five women were preachers' kids, including Abigail Adams, Abigail Fillmore, Carrie Harrison, Jane Pierce, and Ellen Axson, who married another preacher's kid, Woodrow Wilson. In fact, Wilson first met his future wife in April 1883 when he was in Rome, Georgia, tending to some legal matters for his mother. On Sunday morning Wilson attended the local Presbyterian church, where he discovered the pastor was a friend of his father's and the pastor's daughter had "a bright, pretty face."

During his own wedding, on October 25, 1764, John Adams endured one of the most pointed and peculiar scriptural references probably ever used in a New England nuptial ceremony. Reverend William Smith, young Abigail's father, performed the marriage ceremony, and everyone knew his preference in selecting passages that included names of the bridal couple. For instance, when his daughter Betsey got married—also to a man named John—Rev. Smith's text was "There was a man sent from God whose name was John." When his daughter Mary got married, he read the text "Mary hath chosen that good part which shall not be taken from her."

But at Abigail's wedding he read from Matthew 11:18: "John came neither eating nor drinking, and they say he had a devil."[1]

While Lou Hoover left the Episcopal church to become a Quaker after she married Herbert, Dolley Payne was actually kicked out of the Friends church for marrying an Episcopalian named James Madison. Anna Harrison, wife of William Henry, was a very active member of her little church in North Bend, Ohio, and even got in the habit of inviting the entire congregation to dinner on Sundays right after the morning service.

As a child, Hillary Rodham Clinton regularly attended Sunday school, vacation Bible school, and performed in all the church pageants. She even fainted once in an overheated sanctuary while playing an angel during the Christmas program. As an adult she served as attorney for her church and, with her husband, hosted picnics for an adult Sunday school class at the Arkansas governor's mansion. A product of traditional 1950s Methodism, she brought a roar from the audience at the United Methodist General Conference, April 24, 1996, when she opened her speech by saying, "I have to confess to you that I have not been this nervous, with one hundred fifty bishops, someone told me, behind me, since I read in my home church my confirmation essay on what Jesus means to me."

In contrast to the religious behavior of most First Ladies, Mary Lincoln, Florence Harding, and Nancy Reagan dabbled in astrology, to mixed reviews by the American public. Hillary Clinton made headlines in July 1996 because she consulted a spiritual adviser who urged her to consider what Eleanor Roosevelt would say today about the role of the First Lady and then led Hillary through an imaginary conversation with Eleanor.

Several First Ladies taught Sunday school, including Betty Ford, Rosalynn Carter, Hillary Clinton, and Carrie Harrison. In fact, after he returned from his service to the Union army in the summer of 1865, General Benjamin Harrison and his family spent their leisure time thoroughly steeped in church activities at First Presbyterian in Indianapolis. They attended dinners and festivals sponsored by the church. In Sunday school, Carrie taught the toddlers while the general taught the young men's class. Carrie conducted "mothers' meetings" for the congregation, and she served as a special mentor to younger women. Together they both served the church's missionary society.

In 1890, six-year-old Harry Truman entered the Sunday school classroom at the Presbyterian church in Independence, Missouri, and met five-year-old Bess Wallace, the woman he would eventually marry. According to historians, William McKinley met Ida Saxton at a church picnic and visited her regularly on Sunday mornings when he was on his way to the Methodist church and she was on her way to teach Sunday school at the Presbyterian church in Canton, Ohio.

When they lived in Washington, Teddy and Edith Roosevelt often attended different churches on Sunday. He went to a Dutch Reformed church; she went to an Episcopal church, usually accompanied by their children. "But if any child misbehaved, it was sometimes sent next Sunday to church with me on the theory that my companionship would have a sedative effect," he wrote in his autobiography. Edith Roosevelt was known for delivering a sermon on the subject of proper behavior to her children just before entering church, and her husband quotes her as usually ending the homily on the church steps with "No, little boy, if this conduct continues, I shall think that you neither love, honor, nor obey me!"[2]

Instead of leaving the White House for church, Richard and Pat Nixon hosted ecumenical worship services in the East Room. Billy Graham, Rabbi Louis Finkelstein, and Dr. Norman Vincent Peale all took their turns leading services throughout the years. The president grew up a Quaker, and Pat attended Methodist services as a child, and throughout their marriage they never joined one particular denomination. At any given White House service, visitors might range from butlers and maids in the Executive Mansion to the Chief Justice of the Supreme Court. On occasion, the services also were attended by average citizens who wrote the White House and asked for invitations.

A religion writer for a Protestant weekly called *The Independent* is even credited with transforming the expression "First Lady" into the permanent title for the president's wife. As she witnessed the inauguration of Rutherford Hayes, Mary Clemmer Ames wondered if Lucy Hayes might change her hair, her fashion, and her nature in Washington's social climate. In her coverage of the event she pondered whether John Wesley's discipline would vanish in the life of "the first lady of the land."

Wesley's eternal dedication to scripture, reason, tradition, and experience is reflected in the religious lives of many of our First Ladies; however, no theological treatise or biblical passage better reflects their cumulative achievements in the spirit of Christ than the Beatitudes. In turn, the First Ladies' religious stories give new meaning to Matthew 5:3–12. As you read, consider also the concepts of redemption, unity, reconciliation, holiness and wholeness, transformation, wisdom and sanctification—for they are those inevitable elements that rise as naturally from the Beatitudes as Christ's words did from the mountaintop.

The Heart of the First Ladies

While civilization is forever advancing, humankind itself is forever unchanged. You and I as individuals are motivated by the same elemental passions of hope and fear, faith and love. No amount of technological achievements will change that. It was this way for Adam and Eve, and it will be true for the last human left standing on planet Earth.

The spiritual legacies of our First Ladies represent these passions as well. If there was a single voice that *could* speak for the cumulative religious experience of our presidents' wives, it would say: "I was an ordinary woman who stepped onto an extraordinary stage. I discovered the depth of my own fear, the breadth of my own faith. I knew baptism by fire, and I experienced overwhelming grace through the hands of my closest aids and supporters. I was constantly tested by the opposition, and I was often blessed by the kindness of strangers. Ultimately, my gravestone could bear the same mark as yours: I did what I could."

By their examples we are invited to give our best efforts. Through their courage and humor we understand how an individual can influence the spiritual development of a child, a family, a community, a nation, a world. In the spirit of the Beatitudes and in light of all the interviews I've done, all the transcripts, journals, and letters I've read, I believe Eleanor Roosevelt—in her tenure as the longest-serving First Lady, in her humility and in her profound ability to judge human nature—was the most articulate president's wife regarding the spiritual potential of a single life, whether it belonged to a First Lady or you and me:

> A human life is like a candle. It is lit when a baby is born. It reaches out perhaps at first only in the effect even a very tiny life can have on the immediate family. But with every year of growth the light grows stronger and spreads farther. Sometimes it has to struggle for brightness, but sometimes the inner light is strong and bright from the very beginning and grows with the years.

None of us knows how far it reaches but I am quite sure that even a young life that is not allowed to grow to maturity has left behind it influences for good which will grow and broaden as those who touched this life grow themselves.

The great people of the world spread the major light. They leave behind them accomplishments which touch the lives of thousands, perhaps even millions, of people. But they are strengthened by all the little lights and perhaps could never have accomplished their great ends without the little lights which reached out and inspired them in their own particular circle.[3]

—*My Day,* June 4, 1962

In their determination to serve the marginalized, in their dedication to spiritual development, in their personal grace and humor, the legacies of our First Ladies reflect what an ordinary woman can achieve on an extraordinary stage and, more profoundly, they reflect the heart and soul of a nation.

Blessed are the poor in spirit, for theirs is the kingdom of heaven.

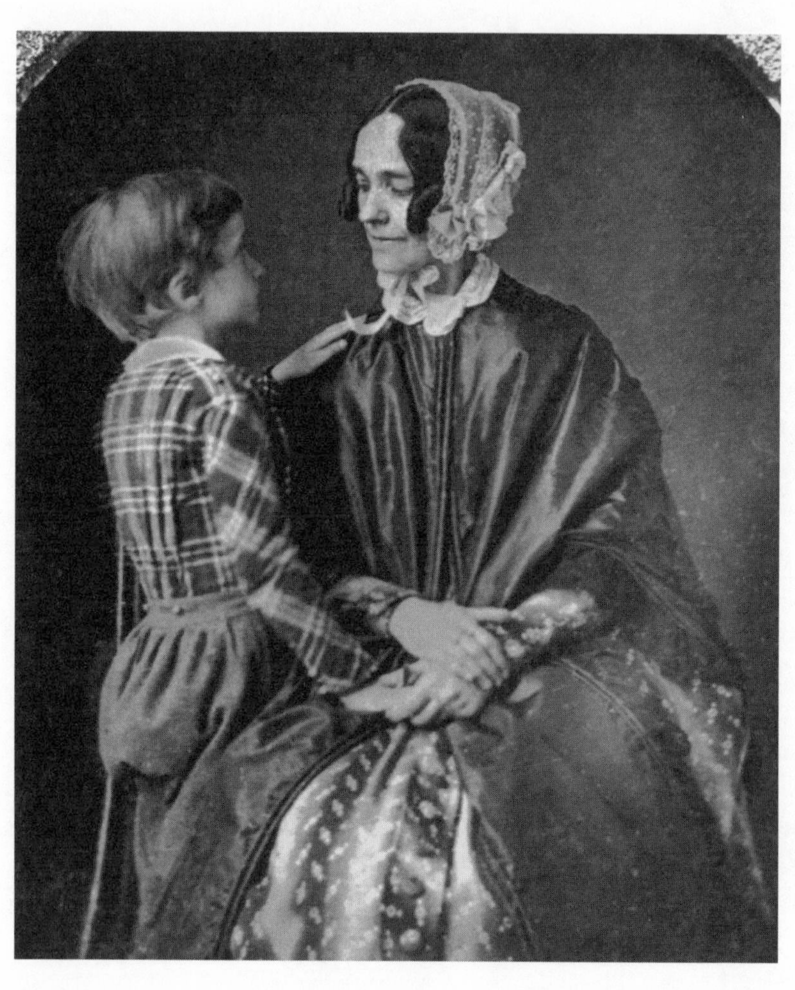

JANE PIERCE

Chapter One

Blessed are the poor in spirit,

for theirs is the kingdom of heaven.

First Ladies Broken by Life

In the Bible, the expression "poor in spirit" appears only in the Beatitudes. However, "spirit" itself is used more than five hundred times throughout Hebrew and Christian scripture, typically as a way of describing the essence of one's soul, identifying an individual's most profound defining characteristics, or holding up a standard for which we should aim. The text consistently illustrates we humans are at our best when we reflect the spirits of truth, life, faith, understanding, holiness, grace, meekness, and especially the spirit of wisdom. These characteristics, in fact, are inevitably linked to rich spirituality, service of others, and joy in the eyes of God. But we also must contend with the spirits of infirmity, fear, jealousy, and the spirit of the world, all of which can drain from one's soul the wellspring within which is the breath and spirit of God. Thus we become "poor in spirit."

Scholars typically offer three possible interpretations for the passage:

Those who are completely broken by life's events and simply not able to function within or contribute appropriately to their roles and personal circumstances. First Lady Jane Pierce is the most heartbreaking example of this.

Those who are determined to overcome their own obstacles and tragedies. Through this interpretation we find some of the most inspiring stories about our First Ladies, especially Betty Ford and Eleanor Roosevelt.

Those who observe brokenness and tragedy in the lives of others and respond with empathy and action. Hillary Clinton articulated this interpretation of the first Beatitude when addressing a Methodist conference: "Take the image we have of Jesus. I can remember so clearly walking up the stairs so many times to my Sunday school class, and seeing that picture that is in so many Methodist churches of Jesus as the Shepherd," she said. "Taking that face and transposing it onto the face of every child we see. Then we would ask ourselves, 'Would I turn that child away from the health care that child needs? Would I say that there is no help for that child because look who he is or look who her parents are?' No. We would take a deep breath in the face of disappointment in our efforts to help and we would continue to try."[1] An elemental and consistent theme in the lives of our First Ladies, this point is interwoven with the concepts of righteousness and mercy as celebrated in the fourth and fifth Beatitudes, and for that reason is developed fully in those chapters.

As it applies most appropriately to the personal and private lives of our First Ladies, "poor in spirit" equals emotional and spiritual depression—feelings of being separated from God, from sanity, and from love as expressed in human affection. As I read the accounts of their psychological suffering, I realized that depression is like an exhausted swimmer treading water in the middle of a river and struggling to make it to the bank. Even at best she may feel she is constantly swimming against the tide. She may see some friends on the shore cheering for her or even trying to throw her a lifeline. Others yell that she isn't swimming hard enough, that she would get it if she were just stronger and smarter.

At worst, depression has terrorized her as she swallows water, struggles for air, and fights an angry, torrential river. She is powerless in the face of gale-force winds and swelling waters. Psychologists will tell you that with depression there are the circumstances we face (the loss, the grief, the fear) and then there are our perceptions regarding those circumstances.

Jane Pierce

Jane Appleton Pierce's life, for instance, was an unresolved Job story. The daughter of a Congregationalist minister who was also president of Bowdoin College, she grew up in a family that was ferociously religious. Her relatives had doubts about Franklin Pierce, especially because his father was governor of New Hampshire. The Appletons took a dim view of politics as a profession, and Franklin was certainly politically ambitious. Jane married him anyway, and correspondence between this unlikely twosome reveals great affection (she was always his "dearest Jeanie") throughout their marriage. They were together thirty years before her death.

It's important also to understand that Jane Pierce believed she was obliged to follow the standard religious training for women of the 1800s and serve as "God's appointed agent of morality," especially in the life of the man she adored. Throughout much of the nineteenth century, America held an accepted religious and cultural belief that women were naturally closer to God than men. Jane felt it was her spiritual and wifely duty to lead her "Frank" away from the immoral world of politics.

Because of her upbringing, Jane held a predilection toward rigid, legalistic views. The faith her parents passed to her did not seem to be one of joy or hope but rather constant instruction on being a good little soldier for God. Their examples were dismissive—sometimes as cold and hard as New England granite—and showed little inclination for self-preservation. Her father, for instance, went to an early, consumptive's grave when Jane was just thirteen because he refused to get more than four hours sleep each night and deliberately cut back his own food in the belief he could get more work for God done this way.

Between this background and the overwhelming devastation she faced, Jane Pierce was one of the most tragic figures to walk the halls of the White House. By 1850, frail health and the death of two of her boys already had convinced her of God's wrath against politics, and when her husband—that great General Pierce who served with distinction in the Mexican War—received the party nomination in 1852, she fainted, then rallied to fervently pray every single day that he would lose the general election. Upon learning her husband would become the nation's fourteenth president, she sank into a frightening depression, and her sense of impending doom could have been more than simply the fruits of her Calvinistic tendencies. This time it may have been prophetic as well.

Before the new president could be inaugurated, the country was rocked by the news that the Pierce family was in a devastating train wreck just outside Boston. Their train car "left the rails and hurled down a rocky chasm," instantly killing Bennie, their only remaining child. The first reports from the scene of the accident indicated the president-elect himself was killed in the wreck, misinformation that swept the country and even forced New Hampshire's state legislature to adjourn that afternoon in honor of its native son.

In what's considered to be the most accurate account, a clergyman named Rev. Fuller wrote about the tragedy, which happened shortly after noon on January 6, 1853. He was one of about forty passengers in the same car as the Pierce family. "The coupling which joined our car with the other broke, and our car was whirled violently round so as to reverse ends, and we were swung down the rocky ledge," he wrote. "For once, I had no hope of escaping death . . ." The train car rolled twice over the rocks and splintered.[2]

The clergyman not only survived but worked into the night to assist the other passengers. He described one woman badly burned but crying in joy that her small boy was spared from death.

> But a few steps from her, I saw the most appalling scene of all. There was another mother, whose agony passes beyond any description. She could shed no tears, but, overcome with grief, uttered such affecting words as I can never forget. It was Mrs. Pierce, the wife of the President-elect; and near her in the ruin of shivered glass and iron, lay a more terrible ruin—her only son, one minute before so beautiful, so full of life and hope. . . . Sacred is the holy privacy of sorrow, and the hearts of those who have suffered can feel what my pen may not describe.[3]

The blow that killed eleven-year-old Bennie struck his forehead with such violence it split his skull, bathed his entire face in blood, and even exposed part of his brain. His parents crawled from the wreckage virtually uninjured and found him as such, an image that forever robbed Jane Pierce of her spiritual peace and her emotional strength. The woman who simply wanted to be a wife and mother in quiet New England, the woman who lost all three of her boys, the woman who never wanted to be a politician's wife and certainly did not like Washington, moved into the White House just three months later.

The March 4 inauguration took place without a celebration ball and without Jane Pierce. She joined her husband later in the month and even then—living in a palace she hated, living a life she felt God hated, and living without the ones who gave her life color and meaning—"was but a shadow in the White House."

She ordered mourning bunting placed in the state rooms indefinitely and stopped Saturday night marine band concerts because they interfered with her prayer hours. Eventually she even tried to rationalize that God had killed Bennie so Franklin would have no distractions. Her mourning paralyzed her in the face of the social obligations inherent in the role of First Lady. She once wrote to her sister:

> The last two nights my dear boy has been in my dreams with peculiar vividness. May God forgive this aching yearning that I feel so much. . . . Mr. Pierce is burdened with cares and perplexities. . . . Little interruptions are very abundant here, and I do not accomplish half I wish to, either in reading or writing. . . . I came accidentally upon some of my precious child's things, but I was obliged to turn and seem [appear] interested in other things.[4]

Mary Custis Lee, granddaughter of Martha Washington and wife of General Robert E. Lee, wrote one of the most gracious reflections on Jane Pierce: "I have known many of the ladies of the White House, none more truly excellent than the afflicted wife of President Pierce. Her health was a bar to any great effort on her part to meet the expectations of the public in her high position, but she was a refined, extremely religious, and well-educated lady."

Rev. Fuller ends his account of the train wreck: "To me the greatest cause of wonder and gratitude is that anyone escaped who was in that car. . . . May the wounded recover . . . and may the bereaved ones obtain that real consolation which the Gospel accords. . . ."[5] Jane Pierce died December 2, 1863, at Andover, Massachusetts, and was buried beside her children in the North Cemetery in Concord. A more merciful passing is hard to imagine, and in her will she provided for bequests to the American Bible Society and the American Society of Foreign Missions.

Her last words were said to have been: "Other refuge have I none." Perhaps only then did she claim the real consolation Fuller prayed for. American history will remember Jane Pierce not for any great achievements as First Lady but instead for the tragedy that swallowed her spirit of hope and joy. In the White House she spent much of her time in mourning, in prayer, and in seclusion, writing letters to her dead sons.

The Public Saw a Brave Face. In Private She Agonized.

In the lives of our First Ladies, depression typically arose—as it does for the general population—from three primary sources: emotional pain (the death of a parent, for instance), physical pain (the spirit of infirmity), and emotional devastation like Jackie Kennedy faced the day her husband was assassinated or for Eleanor Roosevelt the day she learned of her husband's true relationship with Lucy Mercer.

Every First Lady—like the rest of us, it should be noted—has awakened on many mornings to ask herself, "How will I face *this* day? How will I carry out the tasks before me when I am overwhelmed by circumstances?" Rosalynn Carter explains that the most difficult emotional experience for her in her White House years happened when her daughter-in-law Carron and grandson moved out, and Chip's marriage ended. Hillary Clinton hosted the annual Easter egg roll just days after her father's funeral. Nancy Reagan kept her schedule completely intact while preparing for a radical mastectomy in the face of breast cancer. So did Betty Ford.

From the outset, the First Lady's position itself has caused tremendous emotional strain for many of the women who served in its role. Regarding her husband's first term, Martha Washington wrote to relative Fanny Washington: "I live a very dull life here and know nothing that passes in the town. . . . I never goe [sic] to any public place . . . indeed, I think I am more like a state prisoner than anything else, there is certain bounds set for me which I must not depart from . . . and as I cannot doe [sic] as I like I am obstinate and stay at home a great deal."[6]

Grace Coolidge once said to a close friend, "I guess nobody but you has any real idea of how shut in and hemmed about I feel." Ellen Wilson said, "Nobody who has not tried can have the least idea of the exactions of life here and of the constant nervous strain of it all." And Carrie Harrison summed up the emotional pain of watching her husband being publicly humiliated: "Oh . . . what have we done! What have we ever done that we should be held up to ridicule by newspapers . . . cruelly attacked . . . made fun of, for the country to laugh at! If this is the penalty . . . I hope the Good Lord will deliver my husband from any further experience." Upon entering the White House after her husband's election, Eleanor Roosevelt said, "I never wanted to be a president's wife, and I don't want it now. I shall have to work out my own salvation."

Pat Nixon and Eliza Johnson shared the most overwhelming experience of absolute humiliation in the face of their husbands' political downfalls. In 1868 Andrew Johnson narrowly escaped impeachment. The infirm Eliza Johnson was in her private quarters when she learned the news. According to an account by White House servant William Henry Crook: " 'He's acquitted!' I cried, 'the President is acquitted!' Then the frail lady—who looked frailer than ever—rose from her chair and in both her emaciated hands took my right hand. Tears were in her eyes, but her voice was firm and she did not tremble once as she said: 'Crook, I knew he'd be acquitted. I knew it . . . Thank you for coming to tell me.' "[7]

In 1974 Richard Nixon resigned his presidency under the weight of Watergate. In his own account of his wife's devastation over Watergate, Richard Nixon wrote: "I knew how much courage she had needed to carry her through the day and night of preparations for this abrupt departure. . . . She had been a dignified, compassionate First Lady. She had given so much to the nation and so much to the world. Now she would have to share my exile. She deserved so much more."[8] Pat Nixon told her daughter Julie that Watergate was the only crisis that ever got her down, and she knew she would not live to see history reversed on the subject.

Watching their husbands suffer from the physical and emotional strains of the presidency affected nearly every single First Lady at some point. In 1893 Frances Folsom Cleveland participated in a ruse that left the press and even most White House aides believing her husband was taking a pleasure boat trip for relaxation. In fact, he underwent an operation at sea for cancer of the mouth, an event he felt could spark an economic tumult if publicly known. Like the other First Ladies, in public she kept a brave face, saying he simply needed a respite from rheumatism. In private she agonized.

Frances also suffered through one of the more bizarre physical threats ever made against a first family. Her three young girls received such remarkable and often overzealous attention from visitors and tourists that Frances once looked out the window of the White House and saw in horror that baby Ruth was being passed around by a group of strangers while her nurse stood helplessly by. On another occasion, a tourist had to be physically restrained from snipping a lock of Ruth's hair as the child passed through the corridor in her nurse's arms. Eventually, the gates for the grounds were closed to the public; however, in yet another episode three men entered the property with the intent, according to the White House security, of threatening the girls. It was the first recorded threat against a president's child, and the Clevelands received increased security protection for their children.

In her memoirs, *My Turn,* Nancy Reagan wrote about the attempt on her husband's life, which happened March 30, 1981, in Washington. She paced the corridor of George Washington University Hospital waiting for word of her husband's condition.

> As my mind raced, I flashed to scenes of Parkland Memorial Hospital in Texas, and the day President Kennedy was shot. I had been driving down San Vicente Boulevard in Los Angeles when a bulletin came over the car radio. Now, more than seventeen years later, I prayed that history would not be repeated, that Washington would not become another Dallas. That my husband would live . . . When Ronnie first arrived at the hospital, they thought he'd suffered a heart attack. . . . Until they found the bullet hole, the doctors and nurses hadn't understood what was wrong. All they knew was

> that the president of the United States was dying in front of their eyes . . . The bullet missed his heart by one inch. It doesn't come much closer than that.[9]

While her husband served as the Supreme Commander of the Allied Expeditionary Forces in Europe, Mamie Eisenhower struggled so much with her own certainty he would be killed that she lost twenty pounds in a short time, bringing on pneumonia and straining her already delicate heart. Mamie, who had Ménière's disease, which causes vertigo, nausea, and visual blurring, became even more physically delicate in the White House. Once she confided privately to friends, "I think if Ike should become president, it would kill him." In fact, as president he did suffer a heart attack, on September 24, 1955. Mamie later said that after this frightening event she sat in total dread whenever he gave a speech. She was certain he would have an attack on the air.

While all First Ladies suffered emotional challenges, the stories of Louisa Adams, Eleanor Roosevelt, Ida McKinley, Mary Lincoln, and Betty Ford are especially poignant.

Louisa Adams

Louisa Adams, wife of John Quincy Adams, the sixth president, suffered from severe depression, which, she said, seemed to be embodied within the White House itself, where she lived from 1825 to 1829. "There is something in this great unsocial house which depresses my spirits beyond expression and makes it impossible for me to feel at home or to fancy that I have a home any where," she wrote to her son George.

Born in London, England, February 12, 1775, she fell in love, at age twenty-two, with a stiffly principled son of New England, a man eight years her senior who was known for his uncompromising honesty, stubborn nature, famous lineage, and utter lack of warmth. He was a man who said he loved her very much (and meant it most sincerely), but had to admit he loved his country more.

Nevertheless they were married in London in 1797, and from the very start of her marriage Louisa had a witch for a mother-in-law. Abigail Adams, who was open-minded about women's rights and abolitionism, was downright mean-spirited when it came to John's choice in a wife because Louisa was a foreigner. In Abigail's mind that equaled anti-American snobbery, and in one letter to her son she wrote: "I would hope, for the love of my country that the Siren is at least half-blooded." (Louisa's father was an American merchant, but this meant nothing to Abigail and later to critics of the whole John Quincy Adams administration.) Actually, within the minds of the hardy Adams clan, Louisa's greatest shortcoming was that she was *not* from Boston and was treated by many—especially Abigail—as if she should have worn notice of that sin like Hester Prynne and the scarlet letter. Imagine the badge: Louisa, Not-of-Boston.

In addition to these personal challenges, Louisa faced a changing cultural environment which, as one social historian noted, "reduced women to ladies" and offered them a more restricted sphere of activity than even the women of Martha and Abigail's generation had. They were expected to live in genteel anonymity—asked to be ever supportive of their husbands but not allowed an opinion. Shut away from her husband's world of national affairs, she certainly was elemental in John's life but was often reduced to a political postscript, nothing more important than a P.S. you might tack on to the end of a letter.

However, when John served as secretary of state to President James Monroe, Louisa demonstrated she would not remain silent on all matters. In private, urgent correspondence to Monroe dated August 17, 1818, she begins: "Sir, at the risk of incurring the anger of my husband . . ." and proceeds to seek a government appointment for her sister's husband, who John refused to help. "Knowing how contrary it is to my husband's principles to assist any individual of his family," she wrote, "I again repeat that I am shocked at the necessity of the step I am now taking; but my religion sanctions it, and I prefer my duty to God, to my duty to men." Given John's personality, this gesture was nothing less than boldly courageous on Louisa's part.

She and John Quincy Adams entered the White House in 1825, and the role of First Lady was humiliating and devastating from the outset. In a political battle against Andrew Jackson, Adams won by such a close vote, Congress was forced to decide the victor. Henry Clay cast the deciding ballot in favor of Adams, and when Adams later appointed Clay to the post of secretary of state, his own fate was doomed. The Democrats charged bribery and corruption from the start.

In addition to that, John Quincy Adams's plans for national unity and economic development drew indignation and absolute rejection from Congress, and he was quickly and thoroughly targeted as a lame duck. Soon lonely and bitter, he entered his own isolated political world, and Louisa sought refuge by reading, sketching, and—remarkably—by eating chocolates, which she consumed with obsession. Her own depression, she wrote, "passes for ill temper and suffering for unwillingness and I am decried an incumberance [sic] unless I am required for any special purpose for a show or some political maneuver and if I wish for a trifle of any kind, any favor is required at my hands, a deaf ear is turned to my request. Arrangements are made and if I object, I am informed it is too late and it is all a misunderstanding."

Louisa suffered misunderstandings with her husband practically from the first day of their fifty-year marriage. Only in the final years did they find harmony, and as one biographer noted: "Except for her short temper and stubborn spirit, she had little in common with her husband." Louisa herself wrote in one letter: "Hanging and marriage were strongly assimilated." In addition, she suffered several physical ailments, some associated with her twelve pregnancies (which included seven miscarriages). At one point in her life, she remained secluded for weeks. "The habit of living almost entirely alone, has a tendency to render us savages . . . isolation is an evil . . . and one likely to be productive of insanity in a weak woman," she wrote. In 1840 she began writing *Adventures of a Nobody,* an autobiographical account of her life's regrets.[10]

The greatest blow came, though, in 1828, near the end of John's term, when their oldest son, George Washington's namesake, died suddenly at age twenty-seven. Undoubtedly, the White House years were among the worst for Louisa Adams.

Eleanor Roosevelt

For all her stunning achievements as First Lady, nothing is more inspiring than Eleanor Roosevelt's remarkable success at overcoming her own emotional circumstances. Spiritually and emotionally, Eleanor Roosevelt was gifted with sympathy, intelligence, and courage, and she dedicated herself to developing those three. . . . However, joy eluded her often during her seventy-three years of life. "Duty," she once wrote, "was perhaps the motivating force of my life, often excluding what might have been joy or pleasure. I looked at everything from the point of view of what I ought to do, rarely from the standpoint of what I wanted to do. . . . I was never carefree. . . ."

When Cissy Patterson, the editor of the *Washington Herald,* once asked the First Lady how she reached such a level of self-discipline and achievement, Eleanor replied, "Little by little. As life developed I faced each problem as it came along. As my activities and work broadened and reached out, I never tried to shirk. I tried never to evade an issue. When I found I had something to do, I just did it." Patterson concluded, "Mrs. Roosevelt has solved the problem of living better than any woman I know."[11] This is a powerful and ironic conclusion given the tragic elements of her childhood and marriage.

She was born October 11, 1884, to a family of great privilege and pain. Her mother, Anna Hall, had been nothing less than a glamorous socialite, and her father, Elliott Roosevelt, was the handsome younger brother of a future president named Theodore, who served as her godfather. For her part, the plain-looking Eleanor was typically withdrawn, painfully shy, and full of fears. "I was not only timid, I was afraid," she once said. "Afraid of almost everything, I think: of mice, of the dark, of imaginary dangers . . ."

Aware of her mother's constant disapproval, Eleanor was emotionally starved for attention and appreciation. "She is such a funny child," her mother said to friends. "So old-fashioned that we always call her 'Granny.' " First Lady Edith Roosevelt wrote of young Eleanor: "Poor little soul, she is very plain. Her mouth and teeth seem to have no future. But the ugly duckling may turn out to be a swan."

Her mother told her often enough, "You have no looks, so see to it that you have manners." In her autobiography, Eleanor wrote: "My mother was troubled by my lack of beauty. I knew it as a child senses these things. She tried hard to bring me up so that my manners would compensate for my looks, but her efforts only made me more keenly conscious of my shortcomings."[12]

By contrast, her father was warm and affectionate. "I loved his voice, and above all, I loved the way he treated me. . . . I never doubted that I stood first in his heart." He was gone often, though, either on alcoholic binges or in a sanitarium seeking cures for his alcoholism. When Eleanor was eight, her mother died of diphtheria, and just two years later, in the summer of 1894, her father lapsed into a coma after a drunken fall and died—with none of his family around him.

After her marriage in 1905 to her distant cousin, Franklin, she was humiliated by a mother-in-law who ran her household and affairs and a lifestyle of wealth and politics that threatened to swallow her completely. "I was beginning to be an entirely dependent person," she wrote of these years. "I was not developing any individual taste or initiative. I was simply absorbing the personalities of those about me and letting their tastes and interests dominate me.

"I left everything to my mother-in-law and my husband," she wrote. "I was growing dependent on my mother-in-law, requiring her help on almost every subject, and never thought of asking for anything that I thought would not meet with her approval."

Because of Eleanor's insecurity during her early married years and due to her mother-in-law's constant interference, she felt less than successful as a mother. She attempted to offer her children the emotional security and acceptance she never received. "The only thing you can do for people," she told a friend, "is to love them and thereby give them a sense of security so that they know they can come to you and get understanding and forgiveness, even though they know that you disapprove of what they have done." she said.[13]

Eleanor was devastated in 1918 when she learned of her husband's four-year affair with Lucy Mercer, who had served as *her own* social secretary.

According to one close friend, "She was humiliated, hated herself, was unable to eat, unable even to take Communion, although she was the one who went to church every Sunday."

"I do not think I have ever felt so strangely as in the past year," Eleanor wrote in her diary at the end of 1919, "perhaps it is that I have never noticed little things before but all my self-confidence is gone and I am on edge though I never was better physically I am sure."[14]

In 1921 Franklin contracted polio. While his mother wanted him to retire quietly to Hyde Park, his wife urged him to reclaim his political life and move past his physical setback. This was a defining moment in Eleanor's life. As she remarked, it "made me stand on my own two feet in regard to my husband's life, my own life, and my children's training." She felt certain if she had given in to her mother-in-law she would have become "a completely colorless echo of my husband and mother-in-law and torn between them. I might have stayed a weak character forever if I had not found that out."

While biographers typically emphasize her remarkable contributions to the nation's poorest citizens, her tireless efforts for the soldiers fighting World War II, and her bold moves to rebuke racism, Eleanor's decision to throw herself into her political causes also saved her own emotional soul by giving her something to believe in and by building bridges back to her husband, who came to rely on her political independence as well as her opinion.

Eleanor found solace from her closest friends, strength from the work itself, and—when it all got the best of her—she headed off to Rock Creek Park in Washington to sit awhile near the statue of Grief, commissioned by Henry Adams (Louisa's grandson) after his wife committed suicide in a fit of depression. She explained to close friend Lorena Hickok that the hooded figure gave her strength because it represented a woman who had transcended pain and hurt to achieve serenity. "In the old days when we lived here, I was much younger and not so very wise. Sometimes I'd be very unhappy and sorry for myself. When I was feeling that way, if I could manage, I'd come here alone, and sit and look at that woman. And I'd always come away somehow feeling better. And stronger. I've been here many, many times."[15]

Eleanor wrote in a letter to Hickok:

> I'm afraid my reasons for thinking I will probably never be much happier than I am are different from yours, dear. You think some one thing could make you happy. I know it never does! We are not happy because we don't know what would make us happy. We may want something and when we have it, it is not what we dreamed it would be, the thing lies in oneself. . . .

According to one biographer: "She had taught herself how to quiet the longings of the will and achieved an almost Buddhist understanding of how to combine universal sympathy with perfect spirituality."[16]

Broadcasting pioneer Edward R. Murrow once asked her whether she believed in a future life. She said:

> I believe that all you go through here must have some value, therefore there must be some *reason.* And there must be something 'going on.' How exactly that happens I've never been able to decide. There is a future—that I'm sure of. But how, that I don't know. And I came to feel that it didn't really matter very much because whatever the future held, you'd have to face it in exactly the same way. And the important thing was that you never let down doing the best you were able to do. . . .

Of life and death she said, "The only important thing is that you meet it with courage and with the best that you have to give."[17]

Betty Ford

In the two years after she left the White House, Betty Ford developed a growing dependency on alcohol and drugs. She'd been a social drinker all her adult life and had taken prescription painkillers for nearly fifteen years because of a pinched nerve and severe muscle spasms in her neck.

When she faced her addictions squarely, Betty beautifully demonstrated 2 Timothy 1:7: "For God did not give us a spirit of timidity, but a spirit of power, of love and of self-discipline." She overcame her own overwhelming challenges, and of all her contributions, she will be best remembered for her honesty about her problems, her determination to claim victory over them, and her assistance to others facing addiction. In 1982 she founded the Betty Ford Center, also known as Camp Betty, a treatment center for chemical addiction.

Betty entered Long Beach Naval Hospital's Alcohol and Drug Rehabilitation Service in April 1978, and *The Washington Post* ran an editorial declaring that her candor regarding her mastectomy while in the White House gave heart "to countless other victims and prospective victims of breast cancer." The paper went on to say: "Whatever combination of emotional and psychological stress and physical pain (she is arthritic) brought her to this pass, she is, characteristically, determined to overcome it. And she is unafraid and unembarrassed to say so."[18]

In her autobiography, *The Times of My Life,* she confessed: "I was fine when I was in the White House. I had no problems handling myself, despite my present conviction—painfully gained, and offered with hindsight—that I'd have been better off to have thrown away my pills, turned down my glass, and gone for a long walk whenever I was hurting."[19] It wasn't until after she and her husband retired to Palm Springs that her family noticed she was in trouble. Betty had lost her tolerance for pills.

She began to suffer memory lapses. Eventually her family confronted her, and shortly after entering Long Beach, she released a statement that she had been overmedicating herself. "It's an insidious thing, and I mean to rid myself of its damaging effects."

But admitting to alcohol abuse was difficult because her addiction wasn't dramatic. Her speech had become deliberate. She started forgetting telephone calls, and she fell while drinking and cracked three ribs. "I hadn't been a solitary drinker, either. I'd never hidden bottles in the chandeliers or the toilet tanks. . . . There had been no broken promises (my husband never came to me and said, "Please quit") and no drunken driving. I was worried about my children too much to risk taking them anywhere in a car when I'd been drinking. And I never wound up in jail, or in a strange part of town with a bunch of sailors." That is, until Long Beach, she wryly noted. "I love the sailors at Long Beach, because together we embarked on a great adventure. We were all on a first-name basis—everywhere I went, people called 'Hi Betty'—as we struggled with our dependencies and our terrors."[20]

Ida McKinley

Some biographers portray Ida McKinley as an invalid, a victim of epilepsy who completely broke down emotionally after the deaths of her two little girls but went on to give her best effort as First Lady for the nation's twenty-fifth president. Others say that her physical illness, along with her emotional immaturity and instability, brought a constant distraction to her husband, who seemed to spend as much time doting on his wife as he did tending to his presidential duties. Both portrayals are accurate.

Once a beautiful young woman whose vivid blue eyes and thick, auburn hair drew the attention of many suitors, Ida was transformed so much by illness and the loss of both children that during her husband's first presidential campaign in 1896 her low profile brought on rumors that she was "an English spy, a Catholic fanatic, a mulatto, a hopeless cripple overcome by insanity. . . ."[21]

She was, in fact, an uppity American who grew up Presbyterian and married a Methodist. She had fair skin that appeared waxy and mannequin-like to many White House visitors. Eager to prove she was not a hopeless cripple, she usually rebuffed anyone who suggested she relinquish her duties in presiding over the White House's social events.

Consumed by an inner agenda that screamed for constant reassurance, Ida gave in to whining petulance, childish self-absorption, and—when all else failed—she had a distinct way of shrieking, "Major!" that brought her devoted husband on the run.

While some of McKinley's staffers and cabinet officials resented the way she dominated his life, the president himself seemed genuinely to enjoy caring for her. Journalist Charles Willis Thompson wrote: "There is nothing more beautiful than his long devotion to his invalid wife, whose invalidism was not of the body alone. The terrible illness which ruined her health permanently impaired her spirit, but this only made her man her knight; it made him more unselfishly devoted, more tender."[22]

If he thought she was about to suffer an epileptic attack, he guided her away from visitors and to a more secluded area. When she had a seizure in public, he calmly placed a napkin or handkerchief over her head until it ended. Afterward, Ida would resume the conversation, ignoring the lapse and expecting anyone she was talking to to do the same.

On September 5, 1901, when he was shot during a reception at the Pan-American Exposition in Buffalo, his first thought was his wife (who was scheduled to attend the event but canceled because she felt she needed to rest instead). While some men overtook his assailant, Leon Czolgosz, others rushed to McKinley to assess and treat his wound. "My wife," he said. "Be careful, Cortelyou, how you tell her. Oh! Be careful!" George Cortelyou was his secretary.

Ida McKinley outlived her husband by six years. She died on May 26, 1907, just before her sixtieth birthday.

Mary Lincoln

Religion historians often identify Abraham Lincoln as one of our most articulate and insightful presidents regarding spirituality, though he never formally joined any one church, and his early exposure was sporadic at best. During the intense battles of the Civil War in which each side desperately claimed God favored its cause, Lincoln would have none of it. "My great concern is not whether God is on our side," he would say. "My great concern is to be on God's side."

In the eyes of Americans today, Lincoln's maturity, thoughtfulness, and humility earned him universal standing as one of our three best presidents. In the eyes of his political contemporaries in the nation's capital, these characteristics also stood him in total contrast to his wife, who was often described as histrionic, petulant, and clamorous in her need for affection and attention. Always in search of unity, Lincoln once wrote: "Trusting in Him who can go with me, and remain with you, and be everywhere for good, let us confidently hope that all will yet be well." But for Lincoln's wife, as historians have noted in many volumes, things were seldom well from the moment her family entered the White House.

Born in 1818 a privileged daughter of one of Lexington's founding families, Mary Todd nevertheless knew the harshness frontier life could throw upon pioneering families. Losing her mother at age six, she was subjected to a hostile stepmother until the spring of 1837, when eighteen-year-old Mary went to visit relatives in Springfield, Illinois, and decided to stay permanently. Eventually she began seeing her cousin's law partner, Abraham Lincoln, and after a stormy courtship they were married on a rainy night in November 1842 with vows exchanged before an Episcopalian minister.

In the early years of their marriage, Mary managed their household with energy, efficiency, and considerable hospitality for her husband's political associates. Her interest in state and national politics nearly matched Lincoln's, and as his career took him from the Illinois state legislature to the U.S. House of Representatives, she always managed to rise to the occasions with her dinners and receptions, if not her outspokenness and great psychological need to be somebody. Unfortunately, Mary's interest in government also stood in contrast to most political wives of the day. This, along with her one-dimensional view of politics and inability to see past her own agenda, earned her the position of meddling deviant. Many of Lincoln's associates merely tolerated Mary to spend time with her husband.

Her prediliction toward self-deception, conspicuous ambition, and even arrogance left her conflicted and in constant emotional flux: She detested women such as feminists, temperance leaders, and abolitionists who spoke publicly, yet felt she herself deserved public attention. In her almost unwavering state of insecurity, Mary required constant reassurance, yet she carried a sense of entitlement born of her familial background and what she considered her wise selection of a husband destined for greatness. She was painfully sensitive to criticism yet insisted on standing directly beside her husband in the public spotlight.

In 1859 she spent more on one dress than the average Springfield, Illinois, family earned in two months. Upon entering the White House, she depleted a four-year, $20,000 budget for building upkeep in less than a year. She purchased a 190-piece White House china service (royal purple with double gilt) at a cost of nearly $3,200, and ran up a stunning clothing account by 1865 that historians say ranged from $10,000 to $50,000.[23]

As First Lady, Mary's soul was swallowed whole by the circumstances around her, and she actually was as poorly suited to the demands of the role as any other First Lady in history, even surly Florence Harding, whose leathery face was often frozen in arrogant disdain and whose personality seemed an unfortunate blend of mean-spiritedness and genuine lack of intelligence.

When she became First Lady, Mary Lincoln most of all wanted to be her husband's full political partner as well as grand mistress of the nation's most prominent residence. When she moved into the historic mansion, she brought along her expensive clothes, a sizable list of political enemies and some overly ambitious goals of elegance and regal entertaining. She wanted to be remembered for her own achievements independent of her husband.

Even if America had not been struggling through the Civil War, Mary Lincoln's "achievements" might have been difficult to tolerate. However, with the backdrop of Gettysburg, Richmond, and Vicksburg, in a nation overwhelmed by its greatest crisis to date, in a society in which *everyone* lost someone to the violence, Mary Lincoln stood out—independent of her husband—and as an example of one who was absurd, tragic, and worthy of universal disdain.

"I do the best I know how, the very best I can," Lincoln once said to his critics. "I mean to keep on doing this, down to the very end. If the end brings me out all wrong, then ten angels swearing I had been right would make no difference. If the end brings me out all right, then what is said against me now will not amount to anything."

Even ten angels swearing could not have saved his wife from the mental and emotional instability that left her one of the most unfortunate First Ladies in United States history.

Life After the White House

Jane Pierce never wanted to be there in the first place. Neither did Rachel Jackson or Anna Harrison, who openly wished her husband's friends had left him where he was, "happy in retirement." When it came time for their husbands to leave the presidency, Martha Washington, Barbara Bush, and Lucy Hayes were content to move on to the next phase of life, while Eliza

Johnson actually described her intense longing for escape from the White House this way: "It's all very well for those who like it, but I do not like this public life at all. I often wish the time would come when we could return to where I feel we best belong."[24]

But for several First Ladies, departure from the grand mansion and the city itself was depressing and even devastating.

Abigail Adams felt forlorn when she had to leave the role of Mrs. President, and there is wonderful irony here. Over the years she greatly doubted her ability to exercise all the wisdom and power necessary to manage the responsibilities thrown upon her by John's absences. She expressed frequently that she wished she could have been more reserved in her opinions and actions as it applied to matters of finance, family holdings, and eventually national affairs. But she was quickly bored without power, and in one of her many letters she wrote: "It is better to have too much than too little. Life stagnates without action. I could never bear merely to vegetate."[25]

Betty Ford and Rosalynn Carter both felt strongly they had much more work to do on the issues they wanted to advance when their incumbent husbands lost their bids for reelection.

Julia Grant also was devastated to leave. When her daughters asked her what she would say to Lucy Hayes, the new First Lady, Julia answered, "I will say just what Buckner said to General Grant when he surrendered Fort Donelson, 'My house is yours.' " In her memoirs she wrote: "But I did not say it. I quite forgot it and only said, 'Mrs. Hayes, I hope you will be as happy here as I have been for the past eight years.' "[26]

Upon leaving the White House that day, President and Mrs. Grant were met at the train station by many well-wishers, including a Michigan senator who made a point of thanking Julia on behalf of the Republican party for all she'd done for the nation during her eight years in the White House.

> I did not say a word. I simply bowed my head. Oh, Senator! This straw was the lever which opened the floodgates of my heart. I bravely stood looking out, waving my scarf as we glided out of the depot, and when we had passed all our friends I quickly sought my stateroom and in an abandonment of grief, flung myself on the lounge and wept, wept, oh so bitterly. The General, hearing my sobs, came in and with great anxiety asked what had happened. "Oh,

> Ulys," I cried, "I feel like a waif, like a waif on the world's wide common." "Oh," he said, "is that all? I thought something had happened. You must not forget that I, too, am a waif. So you are not alone." This was a consolation I had not considered, but, as I said before, the floodgates of my heart were open, and I wept on and on until I really think if all the tears I shed that night had been gathered in one great reservoir the ship of state might easily have floated safely on their bitter depths.[27]

Julia Gardiner Tyler suffered stunning financial difficulties, especially after the panic of 1873. However, her problems paled when compared to Dolley Madison, whose son Payne spent her money on women, alcohol, and gambling at a rate that often left her financially destitute in her post–White House years. When Congress paid Dolley $30,000 for part of her husband's papers, Payne quickly spent the money, and she was penniless again. Friends began slipping her cash and even stocked her pantry at times. Despite her financial poverty, Dolley Madison was rich in grace. Washington officials made her a frequent honored guest at political events, and for her part, Dolley kept her chin up and her anxiety cloaked, often lending her services to fund-raisers for causes like the Washington Monument and the Washington City Orphans' Asylum.

In the last two years of her life, one particular set of her husband's papers seemed to offer her only financial hope. When her house caught fire one night in the second week of May 1848, Dolley, just a week shy of eighty, yelled, "The papers, the papers first!" She would permit others to carry her out only when she was told the papers would be rescued. Congress finally bought the papers after the fire for $25,000, and most of the money was placed in an account that Payne could not touch. James Buchanan served as one of her trust officers.

Dolley Madison died in her sleep on July 12, 1849. In her final days she gave advice that was poignant, well timed, and offered to a niece who fretted over something Dolley perceived as trivial: "My dear, do not trouble yourself about it; there is nothing in this world worth caring for."[28]

Their personal struggles not only influenced American history, they also revealed the endurance, pain, and vulnerabilities of the First Ladies. For some the story is about a woman who battles her own demons while genuinely trying to make a positive difference in the lives of those around her. For others the story is a Greek tragedy with overwhelming losses all around. The stories in this chapter, though, reflect not just our First Ladies, they reflect our American legacy, the lives of our own ancestors and the unique challenges faced by governmental leaders. Given history's prediliction toward repetition, they even foreshadow the future of the United States. Great lessons are learned from the personal examples of our presidents' wives—great lessons about the heart and soul of our nation.

Echoes of This Beatitude in the Bible

Job 1:21: "Naked I came from my mother's womb, and naked I will depart. The Lord gave and the Lord has taken away; may the name of the Lord be praised."

*Proverbs 18:14: "A man's spirit sustains him in sickness,
but a crushed spirit who can bear?"*

Romans 8:14–16: "Because those who are led by the Spirit of God are sons of God. For you did not receive a spirit that makes you a slave again to fear, but you received the Spirit of sonship. And by him we cry, 'Abba. Father.' The Spirit himself testifies with our spirit that we are God's children."

I Corinthians 2:12: "We have not received the spirit of the world but the Spirit who is from God, that we may understand what God has freely given us."

2 Timothy 1:7: "For God did not give us a spirit of timidity, but a spirit of power, of love and of self-discipline."

Isaiah 11:2: "The Spirit of the Lord will rest on him, the Spirit of wisdom and of understanding, the Spirit of counsel and of power, the Spirit of knowledge and of the fear of the Lord."

Galatians 5:22: "But the fruit of the Spirit is love, joy, peace, patience, kindness, goodness, faithfulness, gentleness and self-control. Against such things there is no law."

First Lady Quotables

"We are carried step by step to endure that which we first think insupportable."

—Abigail Adams

"What you can do is the *best* you can do."

—Rosalynn Carter

"I set out in life with the most elevated notions of honor and principle; ere I had entered it fairly, my hopes were blasted and my ideas of mankind, that is all favorable ones almost, were suddenly chilled, and I was very near forming the horrid and erroneous opinion that no such thing as virtue existed. That was a dreadful doctrine at an age of little more than twenty, but it taught me to reflect, and not build my house in the sand. . . . Popular governments are peculiarly liable to factions, to cabals, to intrigue, to the juggling tricks of party, and the people may often be deceived for a time by some fair-speaking demagogue, but they will never be deceived long; and though they may, in a moment of excitement, sanction an injustice to an old and faithful servant, they appreciate his worth and hand his name down with honor to posterity even though 'that name be not agreeable to the fashionables.' "

—LOUISA ADAMS ON THE FICKLE NATURE OF POLITICS

"You gain strength, courage and confidence by every experience in which you really stop to look fear in the face. . . . You must do the thing you think you cannot do."

—ELEANOR ROOSEVELT

"In the end, what it comes down to is you have to take the responsibility for yourself. Never mind that your wife kept a dirty house, or your mother didn't like you, or your husband can't remember your wedding anniversary. Everybody's had disappointments, and anyone can rationalize his actions. I've been there. Blaming other people for your condition is a total waste of time."

—BETTY FORD

Photo on page 18:

Perhaps the most tragic figure to live in the White House, Jane Pierce lost all three of her sons by the time she moved into the Executive Mansion in 1853. This photo was taken shortly before the death of her last surviving son, Bennie.

Courtesy of the White House Historical Association.

DOUBLEDAY
CELEBRATES
100 YEARS OF
EXCELLENCE

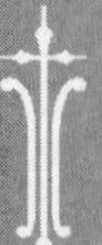

CHERYL HECKLER-FELTZ

Doubleday

NEW YORK LONDON TORONTO SYDNEY AUCKLAND

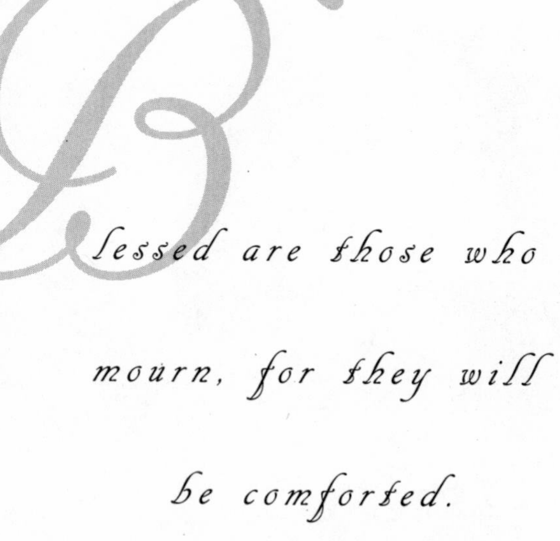

Blessed are those who mourn, for they will be comforted.

Jackie Kennedy

Chapter Two

Blessed are those who mourn,

for they will be comforted.

First Ladies in the Face of Death

For all her achievements as First Lady—promoting the arts, winning the admiration of foreign leaders, restoring the White House—Jackie Kennedy's greatest gift to her country was her response to the assassination of her husband, John Kennedy. From the moment she stepped off the president's plane in her bloodstained suit at Andrews Air Force Base on the night of November 22, 1963, she led the nation through a three-day period of mourning with dignity, grace, and humility. Her exemplary behavior was so effective in its emotional and spiritual impact, young Jackie Kennedy—a thirty-four-year-old widow and mother of two—literally emerged as the most admired woman in the world.

Over the years, eight presidents and three First Ladies have lay in state in the East Room of the White House. The first was William Henry Harrison, whose wife, Anna, hadn't yet arrived to begin her role as First Lady when he died just one month after his inauguration. She never went to Washington for the funeral, and in the end had to wait three months before his body was returned to North Bend for burial. Margaret Taylor and Mary Lincoln were both so distraught, they couldn't even enter the East Room for the viewing or attend their husbands' funerals. Normally one who fell apart easily at simple tasks, Ida McKinley rose to the occasion with such calm and strength, it surprised even her family. In her indomitable fashion, Eleanor Roosevelt treated Franklin's funeral as one more of life's inevitable and difficult events that was to be faced squarely and with dignity. Florence Harding, who will always be remembered as a surly and peculiar First Lady, got up in the middle of the night—unable to sleep—and went to the East Room to talk to Warren. She ordered the casket lid opened, and for more than an hour spoke his name—which she pronounced "Wurr'n"—and concluded at the end, "They can't hurt you anymore."

Throughout history—from William Henry Harrison through John Kennedy—citizens *always* remembered where they were, what they were doing, and who they were with when they heard of the president's death. Those are times when the nation experiences a void in which political differences vanish. In our cumulative grief for the lost leader—who is now bigger than life no matter what happened in his administration—national unity combines with an orphanlike anxiety, and our fears about an uncertain future prompt us to ask simply, "What now?"

Jackie Kennedy

When John Kennedy was assassinated, America wept immediately, but Jackie did not. Like an inauguration, a president's funeral is a great spiritual drama in American history. As one who knew she stood at the center of this drama, Jackie Kennedy drew from a wellspring of inner strength until every detail was carried off, every dignitary recognized, every thank-you written.

With her two small children and the relatively new medium of television, Jackie gave to the nation a magnificent ritual honoring the slain president with stunning images that are still crystal-clear today in the minds of most Americans forty or older: An East Room replicated from Lincoln's funeral; family, friends, and even elderly dignitaries walking eight blocks in the funeral procession from the Capitol to St. Matthew's Catholic Church; the riderless horse; Jackie's innocence at the Rotunda when she leaned forward to kiss the flag-draped coffin; little John's salute; the president's widow and brother Bobby holding hands as they walked behind the hearse.

She wrote hundreds of letters in the days and weeks after her husband's death which demonstrated a remarkable ability to see past her own grief, including this one to Richard Nixon, who lost the 1960 election to her husband:

> You two young men—colleagues in Congress—adversaries in 1960—and now look what happened—Whoever thought such a hideous thing could happen in this country—I know how you must feel—so closely missing the greatest prize—and now for you . . . the question comes up again—and you must commit all you and your family's hopes and efforts again—Just one thing I would say to you—if it does not work out as you have hoped for so long—please be consoled by what you already have—your life and your family—We never value life enough when we have it—and I would not have had Jack live his life any other way—though I know his death could have been prevented and I will never cease to torture myself with that—But if you do not win—please think of all that you have . . .[1]

She received a letter of sympathy from the nation's longest-living president, Herbert Hoover (who died in October 1964 at age ninety) in which he confessed to worshipping her husband as a hero. In response she wrote, in part: "You were always so wonderful to my husband, and he admired you so much."[2]

In her journal Lady Bird Johnson recorded her own images of the tragedy.

During the parade in Dallas, after the Secret Service realized the president had been shot, one agent riding in the vice president's car threw

Lyndon Johnson to the floor of the backseat and yelled to all the occupants, "Get down!"

Lady Bird waited privately with Jackie in a small hallway just outside the operating room at the hospital. "Mrs. Kennedy's dress was stained with blood. One leg was almost entirely covered with it and her right glove was caked, it was caked with blood—her husband's blood." When Lady Bird asked if Jackie wanted to change, the First Lady declined. "I want them to see what they did to Jack."[3]

Throughout the ordeal, Lady Bird kept recalling the death of Franklin Roosevelt. "But this time there is something much worse about it," she wrote. "There is shame for the violence and hatred that has gripped our land. But there is also a determination to help wipe it out!"[4]

For Lady Bird, however, the most poignant and memorable part of the entire ordeal was Jackie Kennedy's strength. "Maybe it was a combination of great breeding, great discipline, great character," she said. "I only know it was great. Her composure is one of the things that keeps on coming back to me."[5]

Jackie Kennedy welcomed governmental leaders from throughout the globe, communicated her gratitude and sympathy to members of the White House staff ranging from her husband's closest aides to the servants. The day after the funeral she invited Lady Bird to tea so she could provide household details to aid Lady Bird's transition. "Don't be frightened of this house," she told the new First Lady. "Some of the happiest years of my marriage have been spent here. You will be happy here."[6]

Crete Garfield

Lucretia Garfield had been First Lady less than three months before Charles Guiteau became convinced God wanted him to kill her husband, James Abram Garfield. It was the summer of 1881, and Guiteau felt the only way to spare the entire nation from another civil war was to make the twentieth president a sacrificial lamb. John Wilkes Booth shot Abraham Lincoln in sympathy for the South; Leon Czolgosz killed William McKinley in the spirit of anarchy, and Lee Harvey Oswald was murdered himself before he could explain why he assassinated John Kennedy. Charles Guiteau, however, believed that just as Christ had to die to redeem humanity, Garfield had to die to preserve the Union.

In fact, three weeks before he shot Garfield, Guiteau attended a little Disciples of Christ church on Vermont Avenue in Washington, where the president had gone with some friends while First Lady Lucretia Garfield remained at the White House, recuperating from malaria. Guiteau later told authorities that after Garfield left to return to the Executive Mansion, he himself went around the outside of the building to determine whether he could have fired on the president during the service through one of the windows. "I could not think of a more sacred place for removing him than while he was at his devotions," Guiteau calmly explained.[7]

Perhaps the greatest spiritual irony in this tragedy is that while Guiteau viewed the president as being religiously expedient, the nation's rapidly developing heartland seemed to cherish the Garfields' spirituality because they represented the values of American Protestantism which staked its claim on the continent decades earlier. Crete and James Garfield "were both devout members of the Disciples of Christ and took their religion seriously; they accepted the Protestant work ethic—dilligence, thrift, temperance, discipline—without question and at times put Puritan virtues above good health," wrote biographer Paul Boller. "And they were devoted to education, prized literature and the fine arts, and enjoyed reading books together and attending plays, concerts and lectures."[8]

The public knew Garfield was a former seminarian. In fact, Lucretia Rudolph met her future husband in 1849 when both were students at Geauga Seminary in Chester, Ohio. (She was the second First Lady to be a college graduate, and she was trained in both Greek and Latin.) Religion historians describe Garfield as a man who was typically gracious and introspective—and as a man capable of demonstrating some rather narrow religious views. He'd clearly won the hearts of Northerners, though, because starting in 1858, while serving in the Ohio state Senate, he effectively articulated the link between religious and civic duty in rebuking slavery and preserving the Union by force if necessary. With his wife's support, Garfield rushed to the colors when Confederates shelled Fort Sumter, and in his service to the Union Army rose from lieutenant colonel to major general on genuine merit.

Crete was thrilled when her husband received the Republican nomination, and described the inauguration as the greatest spectacle she'd ever seen. She was fully prepared to give her very best efforts in her role as hostess during her time in the White House. However, her near-fatal bout with malaria, and Charles Guiteau's act, prevented Lucretia Garfield from making any impact at all.

Presenting himself as "lawyer and theologian," the fastidious thirty-nine-year-old Guiteau held an obsession for politics that matched his fanaticism about religion, and he compulsively consumed every available major newspaper each day. In previous years he had frequented revivals led by nationally known evangelists like Dwight Moody and eventually began his own lecture tour focusing on religion and politics. His efforts as a touring speaker failed, though, because he was often in trouble for not paying his bills.

In history books he is typically identified as "a disgruntled office seeker," a phrase that suggests mere frustration rather than a man who was intense and delusional. Arriving in Washington just four days after Garfield's inauguration with aggressive plans to win an administrative appointment, he left notes constantly for the president, giving advice on how to handle issues, dropped off copies of his sermons, and even attended an open house hosted by Crete Garfield, whom he admired and described as "quite chatty and companionable." In mid-May, Garfield's aides told Guiteau he simply had no chance of an appointment.

The assassin later explained during his murder trial that by June 1 he became convinced that removing the president was the will of God and that he himself was God's chosen instrument. Five days later he purchased a .44-caliber five-shooter known as a British Bull Dog and deliberately selected one he thought was elegant, believing the weapon would eventually be on display in a museum.

On June 18, 1881, Garfield escorted Lucretia to the train station and saw her off to the New Jersey shore, where he hoped she would recuperate faster—and where he planned to join her in early July for a short vacation himself. Guiteau was waiting there to kill the president, but abandoned his plan when he saw Crete, who was pale with illness. "Mrs. Garfield looked so thin and she clung so tenderly to the President's arm, that I did not have the heart to fire on him."[9] On the morning of July 2, however, Guiteau rushed upon Garfield and fired at him while the president's entourage walked through a Washington train depot.

"This is not murder," Guiteau later explained to police. "It is a political necessity."

In the assassin's pocket that day was a letter he addressed "To the White House." It read: "The President's death was a sad necessity, but it will reunite the Republican party and save the Republic. Life is a fleeting dream, and it matters little when one goes. A human life is of small value."[10]

Crete rushed back from the shore to be at his bedside, and when Garfield began talking about how to handle their five children after his death, she said, "Well, my dear, you are not going to die as I am here to nurse you back to health; so please do not speak again of death."[11] Garfield lived for eighty days. His broad, muscular six-foot-tall, 210-pound frame wasted away slowly, quietly, and painfully. His attending physician described him as "a wonderfully patient sufferer."

Meanwhile Lucretia's dedication to her husband brought international attention to the role of the American First Lady. "She has gone on [as] the most hopeful person . . . [so] that it was feared she did not realize the danger," according to one news account. " 'What can save him?' she asked the doctors. 'Only a miracle,' she was solemnly told. 'Then that miracle will be given, for he must live,' she said, and quietly returned to her post at the bed." The account also said, "On every side her praises are heard. . . . As a representative American woman her country people are proud of her. She fitly represents the best qualities of her sex, and is an honor to a nation."[12]

Days of prayer were proclaimed constantly throughout the United States. Daily bulletins of his condition were read in hamlets all over America, and praying for his full recovery became a matter of course during Sunday services. On September 19, 1881, America lost its second president to an assassin's bullet. "It will be no worse for Mrs. Garfield, dear soul," said Charles Guiteau, "to part with her husband this way than by natural death."[13]

But Lucretia Garfield was shattered. "Oh," she cried. "Why am I made to suffer this cruel wrong?" Headlines beatified Garfield by naming him a martyr, a bonafide war hero, and a saint. By contrast, Charles Guiteau became an unfortunate footnote in United States history, claiming his fame as a madman acting out in the name of God. He was hanged in Washington, June 30, 1882.

Lucretia Garfield survived her husband by thirty-seven years, and much of that time was spent at Lawnsfield, the estate she and the president developed in Mentor, Ohio. "There she collected memorabilia about her husband, corresponded with relatives and friends on black-bordered stationery, and followed the careers of her children and grandchildren with loving care," according to Boller. "She also read widely, took notes on her reading, translated Victor Hugo, wrote poetry, gave talks on literary topics to women's groups and began (but never got very far with) a biography of her husband."[14]

In March, 1918 Lucretia Garfield died of pneumonia at the age of eighty-six.

Anna Symmes Harrison

When President Harrison died on Sunday morning, April 4, 1841, the impact for many was the same as when they received the news of George Washington's death. Sadly, Anna was not with him because she stayed behind in North Bend to pack her own belongings and prepare the house for vacancy. In Washington—as well as New York, Boston, and Philadelphia—public and private buildings were draped in black, flags fell to half mast, and businesses closed. President John Tyler transmitted to Anna the Resolutions of Condolences adopted by the twenty-seventh Congress. "My Dear Madame, A great and united people shed their tears over the bier of a devoted patriot and distinguished public benefactor." In her response, Anna Harrison refused to bow to her own agony: "Mingling my tears with the sighs of the many patriots of the land, I pray to heaven for the enduring happiness and prosperity of our beloved Country."[15]

The services were held in the Executive Mansion. The casket lay in the East Room, where the month before Harrison had stood for three hours receiving congratulations on his victory. The casket was covered with black velvet trimmed with gold lace, and over it was thrown a velvet pall with a deep golden fringe. On this lay the sword of justice and the sword of state, surmounted by the scroll of the Constitution, bound together by a funeral wreath. The funeral car was drawn by six white horses. The procession was more than two miles long; in fact, it was even longer than the inaugural pageant.

Anna Harrison remained at the farm in North Bend, outliving her husband by twenty-three years. While fate bestowed her with longevity, she suffered the devastating losses of eight of her ten children by the time her husband even claimed the presidency in 1840. Seven of their children died in adulthood and typically in the middle of rising careers in law or medicine. On a business trip to New Orleans, son Benjamin died in a yellow fever epidemic and was hastily buried by strangers. The family was never able to locate his remains. After the president's death, Anna lost another of her adult children—leaving only one son to survive her when she died in February 1864.

Regrettably, few of her letters survived, including one to her son William while he was a student at Transylvania College. She wrote, in part:

> I hope my dear, you will always bear upon your mind that you are born to die and we know not how soon death may overtake us, it will be of little consequence if we are rightly prepared for the event. I insist that you do not suffer anything to draw your attention too much from your studies, but at the same time take very good care of your health, I would wish you often either ride, or walk out, as I think it be conducive of health. Take also great care of your clothes, and not suffer any of them to get lost. . . . You must write often William to someone of the family, for I shall always be uneasy unless you do, on account of your health. . . . I hope you will not suffer yourself to forget your dear little brother who has left us for the world of spirits. . . . May the God of all mercies bless, protect you and keep you in the paths of virtue.[16]

Margaret Taylor

She was the most obscure First Lady who ever lived in the White House, a woman so strongly determined to have her privacy, she did not attend one single official public event in the mansion, kept herself confined to the family quarters, and became the victim of a speculating fourth estate. Like Anna Harrison, she hailed from a refined East Coast family, married a soldier who would take her into the frontier wilderness, and watched her husband distinguish himself until he claimed the rank of general. Like Anna Harrison, few of her personal papers survived, and in the shadow of more colorful First Ladies, both women often get overlooked. While she was portrayed as poor white trash who smoked a pipe in the White House, she—like the distinguished Martha Washington—was a gentle-spirited Episcopal lady tending to the soldiers who served under her husband and making certain church services at camp were offered and attended.

"Rough and Ready" Zachary Taylor won the election of 1848, primarily because of his victories two years earlier during America's war with Mexico. He served in the army nearly forty years, surviving battles with the British at Fort Harrison and skirmishes with the Seminoles in Florida. He even survived malaria and swamp fever. For her part, Margaret had survived constant moves to new encampments, the dread of tending to wounded and dying soldiers before anesthetics or antibiotics, the birth of six children, and the death of three. Her two youngest daughters, Olivia, a toddler, and Margaret, an infant, died of illness within four months of each other in 1819.

While her father was in command of Fort Crawford, Sarah Knox, the Taylors' second eldest daughter, fell in love with a young West Point lieutenant who was also destined for a place in American history books. Jefferson Davis, who would become president of the Confederacy, found disfavor from both of Sarah's parents because they already had lost their eldest daughter to a military man. As Taylor himself said, "I'll be damned if another daughter of mine shall marry into the army!"[17] Instead, after two years of trying to win over her father, Sarah and the young Davis eloped on June 17, 1835. The young bride died just three months later of river fever, and Jefferson Davis, a devastated widower, and Zachary Taylor, a devastated father, eventually made their peace.

By the time Zachary Taylor entered the White House, he lived through three summers in the swamps of Florida and two years of active duty in Mexico. But in just over one year Rough and Ready died of cholera, and the woman who had survived so much for so long had apparently had enough of it all. She was hysterical at his death, refusing to let go of him, refusing to let his body be embalmed. She could not bring herself to attend his memorial service in the East Room, and when she moved out of the White House she settled on the Mississippi plantation they'd purchased for their retirement. She left no portrait or accurate engraving of herself in Washington and never, according to tradition, spoke again of her days there.

Margaret Taylor slipped into obscurity for the last time in August 1852.

Florence Harding

At the end of July 1923, while on a trip to Alaska that included a goodwill stop in Canada, Warren Harding came down with what was diagnosed as ptomaine poisoning. Canceling public appearances in Oregon, the party pushed on to the Palace Hotel in San Francisco, where he died on August 2, a short twenty-nine months after taking the oath of office.

Attending physicians disagreed on the exact cause of death, and Florence refused to permit an autopsy. It was a decision that later sparked rumors that she herself poisoned him, presumably to prevent him any more pain over the Teapot Dome scandal that hounded his administration and his reputation throughout history. The rumors, of course, were not proven, but after the president's burial in Marion, Ohio, "the Duchess," as she was called, returned to the White House and spent five days sorting her husband's files—burning many of them in a fireplace. Her efforts were both illegal and worthless because Harding's reputation fell so hard so fast after his death that it was difficult to find a Republican leader who would dedicate his tomb.

First Ladies Who Died in the White House

Three American presidents faced the devastating experience of losing their wives to illness while residing in the White House. Letitia Tyler died in September 1842. Carrie Harrison died October 25, 1892, and Ellen Wilson died August 6, 1914. (For details of Mrs. Wilson's death, see Chapter Five.)

Letitia Tyler

As vice president to William Henry Harrison in the election of 1840, John Tyler had the unenviable distinction of replacing the first president to die in office. Just seventeen months after he took the reins (which occurred April 6, 1841), Tyler became the first president whose wife died in the White House. Letitia Christian Tyler was a beautiful woman of delicate health who suffered a stroke a few years before her death. The parents of seven children, the Tylers were married twenty-nine years when she died at age fifty-one.

Letitia Christian was the belle of eastern Virginia—modest, cultivated, educated—when at age sixteen she met John, whose father had served as governor of the state and speaker of the Virginia House of Delegates. Her future husband had graduated from William and Mary at age seventeen and was elected to the House of Delegates at age twenty-one and the United States House of Representatives at age twenty-six. They were married on his twenty-third birthday.

Operating their plantation in his absence, Letitia is credited with such a good head for business, she not only kept the family financially solvent, she allowed her husband greater freedom to pursue his political interests. She was a quiet, deeply religious woman whose husband constantly sought her opinion regarding his political affairs. This was no different in Washington, though by the time she moved into the great mansion, she was frail and reclusive enough to make her a great mystery of a First Lady.

"She accepted the theology of her church as unquestioningly as she accepted all the other standards of her time," according to one biographer. "But her piety came from the heart."[18] One daughter noted that by 1839, Letitia was "always found seated on her large armchair, with a small stand by her side, which holds her Bible and her prayer-book—the only books she ever reads now."[19]

She made only one public appearance in the White House before her death. Her daughter-in-law, Priscilla Tyler, who served as the president's hostess, wrote of the death: "Nothing can exceed the loneliness of this large and gloomy mansion, hung with black, its walls echoing with sighs."[20] The obituary published in the *National Intelligencer* was a perfect period piece with its blushing modifiers, but it is also consistent with accounts by her family and associates: "In the month of September, 1842, died Letitia Christian Tyler. She had been the victim of paralysis for four years previous, but with exemplary patience, had borne its suffering. She was a wife, a mother and a Christian, loving and confiding to her husband, gentle and affectionate to her children, kind and charitable to the needy and afflicted."[21]

Her coffin lay in state in the East Room, and she was taken back to her native Virginia for burial.

Carrie Harrison

Weakened by the coughing spasms and a lung hemorrhage symptomatic of tuberculosis, Carrie Harrison was confined to her bed for the last time in May 1892. Her husband, who beat Grover Cleveland in the election of 1888, now faced Cleveland again in the fall. Throughout the summer and fall of 1892, President Harrison was constantly torn between the obligation to campaign for reelection and the anguishing realization that his wife was probably dying. In the end, he chose to stay by her side, even taking her to Loon Lake, a quiet Adirondack village in northern New York, in an effort to help her recuperate.

At first she seemed to respond to the fresh air and peaceful environment; however, in September she contracted pleurisy, and there seemed little hope for recovery. On September 14 the American public learned that First Lady Caroline Scott Harrison suffered from pulmonary tuberculosis, and while the family tried to soften the blow by saying the issue of mortality remained uncertain, everyone seemed to understand she would soon die.

While her husband knew of her true medical condition, Carrie was unaware and kept insisting that if she could just get back to Washington, she would surely recuperate. In an effort to fulfill his wife's wish, Benjamin Harrison arranged for special transportation to take her the five hundred miles back to the White House. Her train car was equipped with a hospital bed, and an army ambulance met them at the station in Washington to take her home. One newspaper reporter who caught a glimpse of the president at the end of the journey said he was "much afflicted, and his eyes, red from weeping, and with dark rings under them, told the tale of his deep distress and sleepless nights at the bedside of his wife."[22]

Carrie Harrison spent a peaceful last month in her bedroom at the White House while the president and their family maintained an endless vigil. She died quietly on October 25, 1892, just two weeks before the election that put Grover Cleveland back in office. It must be noted that Grover Cleveland declined to publicly campaign once he learned—apparently in early summer—the serious nature of Carrie's illness. In fact, he spent most of that time at his home, Gray Gables, and made but one major address, to some twenty thousand at Madison Square Garden.

The funeral took place in the East Room of the White House on October 27. Standing near her casket, which was covered with chrysanthemums, the president was flanked by his son, Russell, his daughter, Mary, and Carrie's father, Dr. John Scott, a Presbyterian minister who was then ninety-two. Thousands lined Pennsylvania Avenue in respect to the First Lady as the funeral party made its way to the depot for her final journey to Indianapolis. Services were held at the First Presbyterian Church, where she and Ben had both taught Sunday school. She was buried in the Harrison family plot in Crown Hill Cemetery. In the afternoon President Harrison made the heartwrenching journey back to Washington.

His letter of public thanks to the people of Indianapolis read:

> "My dear Old Friends and Neighbors,
>
> I cannot leave you without saying that the tender and gracious sympathy which you have today shown for me and for my children, and much more the touching evidence that you have given of your love for the dear wife and mother, have deeply moved our hearts. We yearn to tarry with you and to rest near the hallowed spots where your loving hands have laid our dead; but the little grandchildren watch in wondering silence for our return and need our care, and some public business will no longer wait upon my sorrow. May a gracious God keep and bless you all!
>
> Most gratefully yours,
> Benjamin Harrison."[23]

The Inevitable Parting

Louisa Adams

One day in February 1848, former president John Quincy Adams collapsed at his desk in the United States House of Representatives, where he served seventeen years as a congressman following his tenure in the White House. His body was carried to the Speaker's room, and his wife, Louisa, rushed to his side. He was eighty-one years old, and he died two days later.

She wrote to her sister, Harriet:

> You may conceive the dreadful shock which I sustained when sent for to the Capitol under the impression that he had only fainted, when I arrived there and found him speechless and dying and without a moment of returning sense to show that he knew I was near him; and thus he lay. I was *forced* to leave him ere the last sign quivered on his lips; it being necessary, they said, for the women to go away. . . .
>
> It has pleased the Almighty in his wisdom to teach me the sad lesson, for so long repining at our continued perseverance in public life. . . . I lived in constant apprehension of its ill effects, and alas, my fears have been too fully realized. But the idea of quitting public life as long as he had the power of acting and the mind to sustain him, were so fixed, it only worried him to suggest the wish. . . .
>
> Dear Harriet, they tell me that it was the act of the Almighty, but oh, can anything compensate for the agony of this last parting on earth, after fifty years of union, without even the privilege of indulging the feelings which all hold sacred at such moments. My senses almost gave way, and it seemed to me as if I had become callous to suffering, while my heart seemed breaking. . . . I wish I could visit you, but I am seventy-three and cannot hope it.[24]

Julia Grant

On the death of her own husband, Julia Grant wrote:

> He seemed to rally for a while in the cool mountain air, and our hopes revived. He wrote on and on in his love's labor. He finished his book about July the nineteen. His work was done, and to our dismay he grew rapidly weaker and weaker, and on the morning of July the twenty-third, he, my beloved, my all, passed away, and I was alone, alone.
>
> For nearly thirty-seven years, I, his wife, rested and was warmed in the sunlight of his loyal love and great fame, and now, even though his beautiful life has gone out, it is as when some far-off planet disappears from the heavens; the light of his glorious fame still reaches out to me, falls upon me, and warms me.[25]

Edith Wilson

In her memoirs, Woodrow Wilson's second wife, Edith Galt Wilson, wrote this about his death:

> My dear one lay in a stupor, but when I would leave the room for a moment and return, he would lift his hand to take mine. Night succeeded day, and the day the night, the hours ticking on unheeded. Thus passed Friday and Saturday, the first and second of February.
>
> The nights were chill [sic], but throughout them both, knots of men and women remained in the street. Sunday, February 3rd [1924], dawned radiant and beautiful. While church bells called people to worship, and crowds were kneeling in the street watching and praying, the frail body which had been racked with pain for so many years relaxed, and the enduring spirit took its flight.

The peace which passeth all understanding had come to Woodrow Wilson.[26]

Lucy Hayes

After leaving the White House in 1881, Rutherford and Lucy Hayes returned to Fremont, Ohio, where Lucy continued her charitable work and even assumed the presidency of the Women's Home Missionary Society of the Methodist Episcopal Church.

She spent her final years in relative privacy, surrounded by family and close friends. On June 22, 1889, Lucy—who often battled high blood pressure—suffered an apoplectic stroke while sitting near the bay window of her bedroom and sewing. Within hours she slipped into a coma, never having a chance to say good-bye to Rutherford and her family. She slept her life away on June 25, 1889, just two months short of her fifty-eighth birthday.

Her husband was devastated, and in his journal following her death he wrote a simple tribute: "She was the embodiment of the Golden Rule."

Thousands of people gathered at Spiegel Grove, their home in Fremont, for the service, which was conducted by Dr. L. D. McCabe, who had been her professor at Ohio Wesleyan in Delaware, Ohio, and the minister who presided over her wedding to Rutherford on December 30, 1852. He also listened to them renew their vows in celebration of their twenty-fifth anniversary, which occurred while they lived in the White House. Two important elements of her funeral seem to best symbolize the grace and mettle of Lucy Hayes.

The first was the hundreds of flower arrangements sent to Spiegel Grove—a fitting response to her death because as First Lady she maintained up to twelve greenhouses at once (they were removed to construct the executive wing during Teddy Roosevelt's administration), and Lucy's skills as a hostess were well proven in her decision to mark birthdays and anniversaries of friends and political foes alike with flowers. Under her direction, many arrangements went out almost daily, and one of the more humorous personal notes she received in the White House came from a member of Congress, who said in essence, "Thank you for the flowers you sent my wife, but I am not married." Lucy wrote back hinting that he should reconsider his marital status because her error surely was part of "some wise plan."[27]

The family of Lucy Hayes—Lucy, who couldn't stand the sight of an undecorated veteran's grave on Memorial Day, Lucy whose last words prior to her stroke were regarding which new rosebushes she'd like to order for Spiegel Grove—was overwhelmed with flowers. It was fitting.

The second symbol came in the form of Rutherford's 23rd Ohio Regiment—now with noticeably thinning ranks and graying hair—which marched on either side of the hearse as it carried her from Spiegel Grove to Fremont's Oakwood Cemetery. The men of the 23rd called her "Mother Lucy," and frequently recounted the story about the green recruit who was told by other soldiers that the "lady in the white tent" would be happy to sew back the buttons that popped off his uniform. He returned a long time later with buttons intact and a wonderful account of his lovely visit with the general's wife. Her absolute certainty that slavery should be abolished and the Union preserved led to her own contribution to the Union Army that was as bittersweet, as demanding, and as dramatic as if she had gotten her wish fulfilled to serve Mr. Lincoln with a garrison of women at Fort Sumter.

Less than four years after Lucy's death, President Hayes himself died of a heart attack and was buried next to her in Oakland, though both were eventually moved back to a small memorial plot at Spiegel Grove.

Eleanor Roosevelt

In the fall of 1962, Eleanor Roosevelt was slowly dying of incurable bone-marrow tuberculosis. Refusing to take her pills and railing against medical intervention that would prolong her life, Eleanor was ready to die.

Biographer Trude Lash, one of Eleanor's closest friends for many years, wrote that she had "helpless anger at the . . . world who tried to keep her alive. . . . She was not afraid of death at all. She welcomed it. She was so weary and infinitely exhausted, it seemed as though she had to suffer every human indignity, every weakness, every failure that she had resisted and conquered during her whole life—as though she were being punished for being too strong and powerful and disciplined and almost immune to human frailty."[28]

On November 6 she signed "A. E. Roosevelt" to a $10 check that was a gift for a friend's daughter. It was a tradition she'd begun during the Depression when she picked up a hitchhiker and helped him get a job. The man said if he had a daughter he'd name her Eleanor. She asked him to just make her a godmother instead. She mailed the girl a gift every year.

Eleanor died the next day.

Bereaved Mothers

> It is an easier matter to conceive than to describe the distress of this Family . . . when I inform you that yesterday removed the Sweet Innocent Girl into a more happy and peaceful abode than she met with in the afflicted Path she has hitherto trod.
>
> She arose from Dinner about four o'clock . . . soon after which she was seized with one of her usual Fitts, and expired in it, in less than two minutes without uttering a word.

This was George Washington's description in a letter written June 20, 1773, of the death of Martha's daughter Patsy.

By the end of her life, Martha Washington had outlived two husbands and all four of her children. As Martha Custis, she lost her first two as infants. Then came a son and heir, Jacky, and later a little girl, Patsy, who was born as her father sank into his grave. In the end, Martha outlived all her children and she and George became guardian and parent to her grandchildren.

Abigail Adams had the dreadful distinction of being the first First Lady to lose a child while living in the Executive Mansion. Her adult son Charles died of an alcohol-related illness during the first four months of his father's term. Louisa Adams lost her adult son, George, the first president's namesake, during the last few months of her already miserable term as First Lady.

Dolley Payne Todd lost her infant son, husband, father-in-law, and mother-in-law to yellow fever in Philadelphia in September 1793. At the age of twenty-five, she was left a widow with one child, Payne. Elizabeth Monroe lost her only son in the fall of 1800. In September, James Monroe wrote to Thomas Jefferson about going to call on a friend "with those condolences which I and Mrs. Monroe were shortly to need for ourselves."[29] It's hard to imagine that anyone could have understood the Monroes' sorrow better than Jefferson. Martha Skelton, married at seventeen, lost her first child as an infant and was widowed by age nineteen. Four years later she married the brilliant young lawyer from the hill country. Together they had six children. Together they buried two. In May 1782 Martha went to her grave with a third, an infant named Lucy. In the end, Thomas Jefferson outlived his wife by forty-four years—and he outlived all his children but one.

Grace Coolidge

President and Mrs. Coolidge suffered the death of their son Calvin, Jr., who was just sixteen, during the presidential campaign of 1924. While playing tennis on the White House courts, he got a blister on his foot which became infected. Blood poisoning claimed his life, and when he died on July 7, 1924, "the power and the glory of the Presidency went with him," Calvin wrote.[30]

Former First Lady Edith Wilson was among those who wrote to the Coolidges, and in her response to Woodrow Wilson's widow, Grace, wrote: "Your note of sympathy and understanding helps the President and me and I am writing to tell you so. We had great hope that Calvin would recover up to the very last for he fought valiantly. It was not for our human understanding to comprehend His plan. I can only bow my head and thank Him for having loaned him to me for sixteen years and ask Him for strength equal to his faith."[31]

Grace's poem, "The Open Door," was published in *Good Housekeeping* in 1929:

You, my son
Have shown me God.

Your kiss upon my cheek
Has made me feel the gentle touch
Of Him who leads us on.
The memory of your smile, when young,
Reveals His face,
As mellowing years come on apace.
And when you went before,
You left the gates of Heaven ajar,
That I might glimpse,
Approaching from afar,
The glories of His grace.
Hold, son, my hand,
Guide me along the path,
That, coming,
I may stumble not,
Nor roam,
Nor fail to show the way
Which leads us home.[32]

Mary Lincoln

In 1850 in America, pulmonary tuberculosis was the most deadly disease, and half its victims were age five and under. It was also called consumption because of the way the illness slowly wasted away the body, and its victims usually alternated between high fevers, violent coughing spasms, and lifeless intervals of exhaustion. There was no effective treatment, and those struck by the disease could linger for months. Parents of small children were subjected to a cruel cycle that forced them to nurse around the clock, offered false hopes for the child's recovery, and then slowly, torturously, claimed its victim.

On February 1, 1850, Eddie Lincoln, aged three, died after fifty-two days of the illness in his parents' home in Springfield, Illinois. The pastor of the Episcopal church Mrs. Lincoln attended was out of town. Rev. James Smith, pastor at the First Presbyterian Church, conducted the funeral and so impressed the Lincolns that Mary eventually joined Smith's congregation, and Lincoln himself attended more Presbyterian services than those of any other denomination.

Shortly after the boy's death, the Springfield *Journal* published a poem written by Mary Lincoln:

Little Eddie

Angel boy—fare thee well, farewell
Sweet Eddie, We bid thee adieu!
Affection's wail cannot reach thee now
Deep though it be, and true.
Bright is the home to him now given
For of such is the Kingdom of Heaven.[33]

When her sister, Elizabeth Todd Edwards, lost her four-year-old granddaughter in the mid-1870s, Mary Lincoln—who already lost her husband and three of her four sons—wrote: "Sweet, affectionate little Florence, whom I loved so well. The information saddened me greatly & rendered me quite ill. I have drank so deeply of the cup of sorrow, in my desolate bereavements, that I am always prepared to sympathize, with all those who suffer, but when it comes so close to us, & when I remember that precocious, happy child, with its loving parents—what can I say? In grief, words are a poor consolation—silence & agonizing tears, are all that is left the sufferer."[34]

Who can say what is a successful transition through overwhelming personal loss when someone very close dies? If there is a correct way to mourn, let's set it aside today. If there is proper behavior in the face of death, let's be hesitant to assume we fully understand it. I am not eager to force any great insights here but will offer this instead: "Do not judge harshly the words of one who mourns" is advice passed down from the ancients. Judge not, but listen patiently and learn, for their words offer the most poignant—and sometimes the most bitter—truths about the human experience. In their responses to death, our First Ladies offer varied examples that range from red anger to peace, childish tantrums to stunning composure. In this, they are just like the rest of us.

Echoes of This Beatitude in the Bible

Psalm 30:11–12 "You turned my wailing into dancing; you removed my sackcloth and clothed me with joy, that my heart may sing to you and not be silent. O Lord my God, I will give you thanks forever."

Psalm 38:6 "I am bowed down and brought very low; all day long I go about mourning."

Isaiah 51:11 "The ransomed of the Lord will return. They will enter Zion with singing; everlasting joy will crown their heads. Gladness and joy will overtake them, and sorrow and sighing will flee away."

Lamentations 5:15 "Joy is gone from our hearts; our dancing has turned to mourning."

Isaiah 60:20 "Your sun will never set again, and your moon will wane no more; the Lord will be your everlasting light, and your days of sorrow will end."

Ecclesiastes 3:4 "A time to weep and a time to laugh, a time to mourn and a time to dance."

Isaiah 61:3 ". . . and provide for those who grieve in Zion—to bestow on them a crown of beauty instead of ashes, the oil of gladness instead of mourning, and a garment of praise instead of a spirit of despair."

First Lady Quotables

"I believe there's a meaning for everyone's coming into this world, that we're put here for a purpose and when we've achieved that and it's time for us to go, the Lord takes us, and nothing can make it otherwise. I believe it, but it's hard for the ones who are left behind."

—Betty Ford on the death of her mother

"How can I tell you, oh my bursting heart, that my mother has left me? At times, I am almost ready to faint under this heavy stroke, separated from thee who used to be my comforter. . . . 'Tis a dreadful time with the whole province."

—Abigail Adams in a letter to John, October 1775. Dysentery had claimed many lives in Weymouth.

"My heart is nearly broke. I try to summon up my usual fortitude but in vain."

—Andrew Jackson

"When the mind is deeply affected by those irreparable losses which are incident of humanity the good Christian will submit without repining . . . but in the severest trials we find some alleviation to our grief in the sympathy of sincere friends . . ."

—MARTHA WASHINGTON ON THE DEATH OF HER HUSBAND

"The story is over."

—ELEANOR ROOSEVELT ON THE DEATH OF HER HUSBAND

Photo on page 48:

In 1963 the nation was devastated by the news of President John F. Kennedy's assassination, but was comforted by the dignity and grace of his young widow, walking here behind her husband's casket with her brother-in-law, Robert Kennedy.

UPI/Corbis-Bettmann

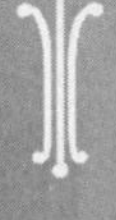

Blessed are the meek,

for they will inherit

the earth.

Lady Bird Johnson

Chapter Three

Blessed are the meek,

for they will inherit the earth.

The Meek First Ladies

There is a dangerous woman in the White House. The First Lady is overeducated, overopinionated, and holds far too much influence with her husband. She is a strong-willed social reformer, and—to those who know her best—a smooth political operator.

She regularly attends Foundry Methodist Church in Washington. She is redefining women's role in America. Her husband's foes may ridicule her, but would be foolish to underestimate her. And she has a very popular cat named . . . Siam.

Siam?

Did I mention it's 1877? We're talking about Lucy Webb Hayes. A devout, well-bred Ohio-born woman, the wife of and indefatigable hostess for the nation's nineteenth president rang up a list of White House firsts.

The first to hold a college degree. The first to bring the children's Easter egg roll to the White House. The first to travel to the West Coast.

Armed with her college degree and saddled with the most disputed presidential election results in American history (it was outright political thievery), Lucy entered the White House as one of the most reviled First Ladies of the 1800s. In this century, only Eleanor Roosevelt and Hillary Clinton have stirred a greater degree of personal and political animosity than that which greeted "Lemonade Lucy," the woman credited with bringing temperance to the White House.

Lucy Hayes is also the perfect example of meekness, and there is a wonderful irony here: As a spiritual characteristic, meekness is as misunderstood by us today as Lucy was by our nation one century ago. We as individuals are wary of the word "meekness" because it is a tired and discarded trait typically interpreted as its rhyming antonym "weakness." Poorly taught by some religious leaders, it has even been used over the centuries as a weapon of submission for both women and African Americans.

The America that evaluated Lucy Hayes in 1876 was a nation still badly wounded by a civil war and clearly confused by a presidential election in which a Democrat won by half a million popular votes but a Republican took office. While many Southerners suffered through financial devastation, Lucy Hayes grew up in wealth and then married wealth, but no historian ever accused her of flaunting it. Washington's political elites who had just had eight years of the hard-drinking Grant administration now faced Rutherford and Lucy Hayes, who both learned in childhood the Methodist pledge of temperance. They first met, in fact, at Ohio Wesleyan University while she was a student there and he came to campus for a temperance meeting.

Despite our initial misgivings about "meekness," throughout scripture it is almost always associated with strong characteristics such as godliness, temperance (moderation), self-discipline, and applied wisdom. The fruits of meekness include patience, determination, discernment, and a sense of personal grace. Despite the nation's initial misgivings about her, Lucy Hayes was an extremely successful First Lady because she possessed these traits.

Meekness is more complex, I believe, than the concepts raised by the other Beatitudes. Eleanor Roosevelt once befriended a hitchhiker and helped him get a job. That is an example of mercy that was just summarized in one sentence. But meekness is not so easy because it actually represents an intersection that joins several other spiritual concepts.

Of the hundreds of names found in scripture, only Moses and Christ himself are described as "being meek." Within the context of scripture, meekness is a path to greater spiritual strength, to personal salvation, to sustenance for those who are "lifers" in the army of God. Meekness is permanently linked with lifetime dedication to Christ's teachings, with a constant search for the will of God. It implies devotion to scriptural study. It means making the specific decision to express love and support when judgmental retribution is more tempting. Though it is often interpreted as "acquiescing," "giving in," or "staying silent," a more accurate understanding of the word is "thoughtful response not produced in anger or crass cleverness."

Meekness is not about romantic, dramatic, or exciting adventures. It is inevitably tied to responsibility and duty; to patience and tenure; to building a portfolio of service. I sometimes wonder if Christ's dedicating the Earth to the meek isn't more a promise to the Creator than it is a promise to humans. Who better to care for the world than the wisest, most patient elders?

Lucy Webb was born in 1831 in Ross County, Ohio, the third child and only daughter of Dr. James Webb, a prominent Chillicothe physician, and his wife, Maria. Lucy was just two years old when her father died while trying to rein in a cholera epidemic in Kentucky—an outbreak that also killed both his parents and his brother. She came from a long line of fiery reformers who dedicated their money and position to social justice. Her grandfather, Isaac Cook, was an Ohio judge and legislator who campaigned tirelessly for temperance and public education. Under his influence, Lucy received an unusually thorough education for a young woman of her day, eventually getting a degree from Wesleyan Female College, a Methodist school in Cincinnati.

Lucy and Rutherford were married December 30, 1852, and from the start she expressed strong views on politics, believing as she did, for instance, that the newly galvanized Republican party was the social salvation of the nation. She considered slavery an abomination and the greatest social evil of our civilization. Lucy often said she wished she could have served

Mr. Lincoln at Fort Sumter with a garrison of women. Rutherford wryly noted that instead, she had to content herself with his enrollment into the Union Army. In fact, Lucy Hayes was married to the leader of the "Fighting 23rd," a bona fide war hero wounded several times and one who had his horse shot out from under him twice.

Rutherford Hayes climbed to the rank of major general, and when his political supporters and friends drafted him into the race for the United States House of Representatives in the fall of 1864, he spat back fire: "An officer fit for duty who at this crisis would abandon his post to electioneer for a seat in Congress ought to be scalped."[1] It was a classic Lucy perspective as well. Instead, Rutherford won the seat without ever leaving his troops, an election that began the political journey that ended in the White House in 1877.

In her report of the inaugural of Rutherford Hayes for the Protestant weekly newspaper *The Independent,* Mary Clemmer Ames referred to Lucy as "first lady of the land." The title stuck, ending such encumbered phrases as "Lady Presidentress," and actually influencing the role itself. But I believe Ames got it backward: "Lady first" is the most accurate description of Lucy Hayes because her defining belief that a woman must always remain a lady was as elemental to her being as the coronet braid hairstyle of her youth and the rheumatism of her adulthood. It was a mantle she wore with comfort.

According to Edith Mayo, curator emeritus of the First Ladies Exhibit at the Smithsonian Institution in Washington, D.C., "She was hailed as sort of an exemplar of the new woman in the late nineteenth century, and part of that image included nurturing a larger community. Accomplishments in her own right never did overshadow her husband or look self-aggrandizing, but she proved you no longer had to be frail and fainting to be a true woman."[2]

Fainting indeed.

When her husband was elected governor of Ohio in 1867, Lucy Hayes immediately dedicated herself to the orphans of Ohio's soldiers who served the Union Army during the Civil War. Appalled when she learned the Democrat-controlled state legislature refused to create what she considered a desperately needed orphanage, Lucy—with her sweet smile and piercing brown eyes—began covertly twisting arms in an impressive round of backroom politics until the Ohio Senate passed the bill by a single vote. The building was constructed and adequately furnished. In her efforts she was strongly supported by the Grand Army of the Republic, and Rutherford proudly noted that Lucy "ransacked" Columbus for money, books, and gifts to make certain each child had at least one present for the first public event, a Christmas party.

In her forceful if private way, Lucy pushed the completion of the Washington Monument and supported the National Deaf Mute College and Hampton College, which had been created in 1868 to educate African Americans.

Lucy's destiny in United States history, however, is forever linked to temperance, and few Americans understand the love-hate relationship she shared with the movement's leaders, who created a dizzying cycle of insulting Lucy, thanking her, rejecting her, honoring her, and insulting her. They failed to understand that Rutherford demanded the no-liquor policy, not Lucy. She believed in temperance as it applied to her own life but refused to espouse her beliefs in social events, in large part, because of her many close friends and supporters who did drink. In a tribute to Lucy—and with personal knowledge of her wit and charm—Mark Twain once wrote: "Total Abstinence is so excellent a thing that it cannot be carried to too great an extreme. In my passion for it, I even carry it so far as to totally abstain from Total Abstinence itself."[3]

To the end of her life she was known for her wit, humor, and remarkable capacity for work. "Everyone praises the way Mrs. Hayes plasters down her hair and enthuses over her Columbus cut dresses," wrote one reporter shortly after Lucy reached the White House. "In ninety days she will be picked to minute shreds." This prompted Lucy to write privately to one son: "You see, dear Birch, without intending to be public [a public figure], I find myself—for a quiet, 'mind her own business' woman—rather notorious."[4]

Martha Washington

Martha Washington did not want to be First Lady of any country. She'd already endured years of separation from her husband because of the war, and she longed for a quiet retirement to the fields and family at Mount Vernon. But it was not to be.

Martha once referred to her time as the president's wife as "the lost days," and to one niece she wrote that she felt poorly suited to be in the middle of such pomp and so many societal expectations. "I have not had one half hour to myself since the day of my arrival," she wrote in one letter. Despite these frustrations, Martha remained dedicated to her work just as her husband was.

"I do not . . . feel dissatisfied with my present situation," she wrote.

> No. God forbid! For everybody and everything conspire to make me as contented as possible in it. Yet I know too much of the vanity of human affairs to expect felicity from the splendid scenes of public life. I am still determined to be cheerful and to be happy, in whatever situation I may be; for I have also learned from experience that the greater part of our happiness or misery depends upon our dispositions, and not upon our circumstances. We carry the seeds of the one or the other about with us in our minds where ever we go.[5]

In August 1774, Patrick Henry and Edmund Pendleton stopped at Mount Vernon to spend the night and then leave the next morning with George for Philadelphia and the convening of the Second Continental Congress, which would determine the future of the colonies. They all suspected war was inevitable. "She seemed ready to make any sacrifice, and was very cheerful, though I know she felt very anxious," Pendleton later wrote about Martha.

Abigail Adams

Abigail Adams expressed similar views about life as Martha Washington. "I am determined to be very well pleased with the world and wish well to all its inhabitants. Altho in my journey through it, I meet with some who are too selfish, others too ambitious, some uncharitable, others malicious and envious [all are opposites of meekness], yet these vices are counterbalanced by opposite virtues . . . and I always thought the laughing philosopher a much wiser man than the sniveling one."[6]

No doubt one reason Abigail frequently questioned her own "patience, prudence and discretion" is that she was often forced to handle traditionally male responsibilities and did so with such skill, she caused herself guilt at not being more ladylike. While John Adams was away—as he was often on the court circuit and then in national service—Abigail managed the household, ran the farm, saw to their four children's education, handled the family's finances, and even expanded their holdings. At first she sought her husband's opinion on every action. She received so much encouragement from him regarding her success that it led to a mutual respect, and he, in turn, sought her opinion on political matters.

In fact, while scripture reports the fruits of meekness to be patience, endurance, and kindness, in the lives of First Ladies, meekness typically has created mutual respect and partnership within their marriages, effective responses to the needs of America's poor or powerless citizens, and clarity of mission. While meekness may be misinterpreted as passivity or shyness, the lives of First Ladies—like the New Testament implication—actually reveal a sense of responsibility and urgency as well as personal action.

Lady Bird Johnson

One Sunday in the fall of 1967 President Lyndon Johnson and his wife, Lady Bird, were sitting in the front pew of the Bruton Parish Episcopal Church in Williamsburg, Virginia, when the rector launched into an abrasive sermon that had nothing to do with scripture but focused instead on the state of the union. In short order, he managed to cover civil rights, disorder in the streets, and the general upheaval of the nation.

As bad as that was, it got worse. Lady Bird Johnson, writing of this exasperating episode in her book, *A White House Diary,* said she froze in her seat when she heard him say, " 'And then there is the question of Vietnam.' " The pastor, Reverend Cotesworth Pinckney Lewis, said the nation was mystified by news accounts that the men fighting there were inhibited by misinformation, poor military directives, and inadequate equipment. He said that at the same time America pledged her loyalty to the cause, she was clearly asking, "Why are we there?"

Appalled by the pastor, Mrs. Johnson said, "I turned to stone on the outside and boiled on the inside." As the Johnsons left the church that day, there was the inevitable melee of flashing cameras, casual tourists, and visitors waving to them—and there stood the pastor with his hand extended. "Be it said for my husband that he shook hands briefly with a smile while I said, 'The choir was beautiful,' " she wrote in her journal.

According to Mrs. Johnson, the rector then distributed copies of his sermon to the press and explained that criticism was actually the furthest thing from his mind. He hoped the president took no offense and instead understood it in the spirit of honest and reasonable give-and-take. He also told the press he delivered this particular sermon because it was not every day that one had the privilege of speaking his mind to the president of the United States.

Meanwhile Lyndon Johnson looked down at his wife with a wry smile and said, "Greater love hath no man than that he goes to the Episcopal church with his wife!"[7]

Historians usually cut to the chase when describing the political prowess of Lyndon Johnson: He was single-minded, charming, hungry, focused, and usually impatient. In the fall of 1934, when he met Claudia Taylor in Austin, Texas, while on assignment as a legislative aide to Congressman Richard Kleberg, he knew immediately this was the woman he wanted for his wife. Lady Bird—always a shy, sensitive, and remarkably calm woman—had just graduated from the University of Texas with a degree in journalism.

He was typical Johnson. He told her many facts about his own life that she considered extraordinarily direct for a first conversation. He told her how many years he had been teaching, his ambitions, his background. He even told her how much he earned as a congressman's aide and how much insurance he had, in addition to all sorts of tales about his family. Johnson was giving her the complete picture of his past, as well as his goals for the future, because he wanted her for his own.

He returned to Washington, where he wrote or telephoned her daily. On his next visit to Texas seven weeks later he arrived at her doorstep with a rather intense proposal: "Let's get married. Not next year, after you've done over the house, but about two weeks from now, or right away. If you say no, it just proves that you don't love me enough to dare to marry me. We either do it now, or we never will."[8]

The next week they were married—on November 17, 1934. Historians love to say that before Dolley Payne first met James Madison, he looked like a man headed to a funeral. That changed significantly after their marriage, and her sense of grace helped him to develop social skills no one knew he had. In that same spirit, Lady Bird proved to be the perfect companion for Lyndon Johnson. She gracefully hosted the throngs he invited to their house, managed his personal affairs, and tolerated his outbursts with a calmness some around her simply could not understand. In the White House she championed highway beautification, environmental issues, and civil rights. But one of her greatest contributions to her husband's presidency was the dignity and balance she offered to a nation struggling with the death of John Kennedy, an escalating war in Vietnam, and civil rights. She helped her husband with these struggles as well.

One of the poignant examples of Lady Bird's undying support of her husband came on August 25, 1964, the day after the Democratic National Convention opened in Atlantic City. It had been just nine months since the assassination of John Kennedy, and Johnson saw the nation through as smooth a transition as possible but now sat in the White House with tremendous doubts about the future. Finally, in total exasperation, he took out a yellow pad and wrote an impassioned statement indicating his withdrawal from the political race before him. It read in part: "For nine months I've carried on as effectively as I could. . . . The times require leadership about which there is no doubt and a voice that men of all parties, sections and color can follow. I have learned after trying very hard that I am not that voice or that leader."[9]

He showed the draft to Lady Bird, and her thoughtful response came in the form of this letter:

> Beloved—
>
> You are as brave a man as Harry Truman—or FDR—or Lincoln. You can go on to find some peace, some achievement amidst all the pain. You have been strong, patient, determined beyond any words of mine to express. I honor you for it. So does most of the country. To step out now would be *wrong* for your country, and I can see nothing but a lonely wasteland for your future. Your friends would be frozen in embarrassed silence and your enemies jeering.
>
> I am not afraid of *Time* or lies or losing money or defeat.

In the final analysis I can't carry any of the burdens you talked of—so I know it's only your choice. But I know you are as brave as any of the thirty-five.

I love you always.
Bird[10]

Johnson credited his wife with his decision to stay in the race. He went to the Democratic Convention, accepted the nomination, and won the race in 1964.

In the White House Lady Bird Johnson contributed significantly to the cause of civil rights. While Southern leaders were chivalrous to her when she campaigned on her train, the *Lady Bird Special,* protesters openly displayed signs that read FLY AWAY BLACK BIRD! Despite a bomb threat, challenges from the Ku Klux Klan, and constant catcalls whenever she spoke, Lady Bird stood firm for the cause. She would even say to angry protesters, "In this country we have many viewpoints. You are entitled to yours. Right now, I am entitled to mine."

She also was harassed constantly for the escalation of the Vietnam War and often heard the chant "Hey, hey, LBJ, how many boys did you kill today?" While her husband developed a theory that many of his political obstacles were part of a conspiracy, Lady Bird herself responded with a quiet dignity that strengthened her husband, daughters, and even the White House staff.

Edith Roosevelt

"I take the keenest pride in seeing Mrs. Roosevelt at the head of the White House," President Theodore Roosevelt once wrote to William Howard Taft. "She is a gentlewoman, who gives to all the official life an air of gracious and dignified simplicity, and who with it all is the ideal of a good American wife and mother who takes care of her six children in the most devoted manner. Mrs. Roosevelt comes a good deal nearer my ideal than I do myself."

The nation's twenty-sixth president was not alone in his views, and in the history of our nation, Edith Roosevelt may have been the media's favorite First Lady of all. Like Eliza Johnson in 1865 and Lady Bird Johnson in 1964, she entered the White House after the assassination of a president (Chester Arthur was widowed when he replaced James Garfield). William McKinley was shot during the Pan-American Exposition in Buffalo, New York, on September 7, 1901, and died several days later.

"I suppose in a short time I shall adjust myself to this," she wrote after her husband took the oath of office, "but the horror of it hangs over me, and I am never without fear for Theodore. The secret service men follow him everywhere. I try and comfort myself with the line of the old hymn, 'Brought safely by His hand thus far, why should we now give place to fear?' "[11] Returning home to Sagamore Hill after McKinley's funeral just long enough to pack up her family for the move to Washington, she found a symbol of just what impact the White House could have on her children. Entering the nursery, she discovered her children's dolls lined up on the bed—each one wearing a black mourning armband in honor of the fallen president.

After moving into the White House, Edith quickly adjusted her life around her husband and children. She disliked all news accounts about her family, saying, "One hates to feel that all one's life is public property." Edith maintained a ritual of spending at least thirty minutes reading and talking to her children before dinner every evening. President Roosevelt often entered the room, kissed her hand, and then sat to listen to her read as well. When she finished, he would pull the children onto the floor for some wrestling. That was *his* ritual before dinner.

Edith Roosevelt rose to the social role of president's wife with such style and grace, she managed her six boisterous, outgoing, prank-loving children, her indefatigable, boisterous, prank-loving husband, and one of the most daunting reception and entertainment schedules of any First Lady in history. With Dolley Madison's flair for putting people at ease, with Patricia Nixon's regal, quiet dignity, and with youthful good looks that could have rivaled Jackie Kennedy's, Edith was almost the dead opposite of her predecessor, the mousy and difficult Ida McKinley.

United States Senator Marcus Alonzo Hanna was the archrival of Theodore Roosevelt; however, his respect for the First Lady was near legendary. After watching a small boy stand in Dupont Circle speaking to the First

Lady and her son Quentin, Hanna waited until the Roosevelts' carriage pulled away and then spoke firmly to the boy: "You! You ought take your hat off when any woman speaks to you. When Mrs. Roosevelt speaks to you, keep it off a week!"[12]

The Washington press discovered during Teddy Roosevelt's term that the president's six children and their pets made great stories. In the spring of 1903, nine-year-old Archie Roosevelt missed the annual Easter games, when thousands of children descend on the White House grounds with baskets of hard-boiled eggs, which they roll down the gently sloping hills on the grounds. Sick with both measles and whooping cough, Archie also was saddened by the death of his fox terrier, Jack Dog. To boost his brother's spirits, six-year-old Quentin Roosevelt recruited a White House footman to help him haul Archie's calico pony into the elevator and up to the family quarters. If the 350-pound animal was nervous about the trip, the family seemed to think the outcome was worthwhile, for Archie got back on his feet in short order. Soon, in fact, Archie would have another canine—a seafaring mongrel named Skip who was thrilled to go sailing with his young master. The Roosevelt children also had flying squirrels, guinea pigs, and a pony named General Grant.

Tom Quartz was a kitten who once seized Joe Cannon, the speaker of the United States House of Representatives, by the ankle as he descended the grand staircase of the White House. The Roosevelts' son Kermit had a kangaroo rat who was fed sugar cubes at the breakfast table. Their daughter Alice had an emerald-green snake named Emily Spinach, which she pulled from her purse at parties. The whole family heard frequently from Eli the macaw and Loretta the parrot, who filled the hallways of that stately Executive Mansion with their squawking.

Edith tolerated the menagerie in good humor while the president urged it along steadily. In his autobiography he proudly noted one unique encounter between his youngest son, Archie, a visiting reptile, and a member of the United States Congress. Archie had been visiting a pet store, when the owner told the boy to take a king snake home for a while (lending pets was common with the owner). Slipping the snake inside his coat, Archie raced home and was so excited he rushed into his father's office to show him the treasure—correctly judging that the president would be thrilled with the visitor. Representative Pete Hepburn was in Roosevelt's office, discussing with the president a bill pending on railroad rates. Archie came bounding in and then immediately started squirming, tickled by a snake now crawling down his sleeve. The congressman reached down to help the boy with his coat "and then jumped back with alacrity as the small boy and the snake both popped out of the jacket."[13]

The family also had a young black bear (not on White House property) which the children named Jonathan Edwards, Roosevelt wrote, "partly out of compliment to their mother, who was descended from that great Puritan divine, and partly because the bear possessed a temper in which gloom and strength were combined in what the children regarded as Calvinistic proportions."[14] Just one month after the pony went up the elevator, the president brought the children a pet badger named Josiah from one of his trips out west. More than one historian has noted that—at certain moments—Edith had not six children, but *seven.*

Whatever charges Teddy Roosevelt's enemies made against his family, dullness was never one of them. As chief usher Ike Hoover wryly noted, "A nervous person had no business around the White House in those days. He was sure to be a wreck in a very short time."[15] Yet Edith managed this household with warmth and dignity. She was a patient and willing companion in most of her husband's adventures. She was a tonic for his restlessness, and she remained determined to make the best of whatever charged toward her—whether it was a son on roller skates in the East Room or her husband with more unexpected guests for lunch.

Unlike the other First Lady named Roosevelt, Edith did not recognize the role of social *worker* within the primary duties of the president's wife. Still, she made two enduring contributions when she created the White House China Collection and—even more important—the gallery of portraits of First Ladies. These two elements highlighted the contributions of her predecessors and provided tangible evidence that First Ladies offered a unique influence on the life of the nation.

"I do not think my eyes are blinded by affection when I say that she has combined to a degree I have never seen in any other woman the power of being best of wives and mothers, the wisest manager of the household, and at the same time the ideal great lady and mistress of the White House," wrote Teddy Roosevelt.[16]

Just three weeks after her husband left office, Edith endured a difficult one-year separation from him while he and son Kermit went to Africa hunting big game. They were reunited in Europe and toured several countries there before returning to the United States. The former president immediately became embroiled in Republican politics, and Edith once again faced upheaval as he squared off for the presidency in 1912 against his own handpicked successor, William Howard Taft, by creating a third party, officially known as Progressive Republicans but affectionately called the Bull Moosers.

While campaigning in Milwaukee, Roosevelt became the target of an assassination attempt. The bullet struck his spectacle case first, a fate that surely spared his life. Wounded and shaken, Roosevelt insisted on making his scheduled speech that evening—a speech lasting ninety minutes—and Edith eventually caught up with him in a Chicago hospital. "We are against his politics," noted one national paper, "but we like his grit."

Edith Roosevelt proved she had grit as well. "That sedate and determined woman, from the moment of her arrival . . . took charge of affairs," wrote correspondent Charles Willis Thompson. "The moment she arrived a hush fell on TR . . . he became *as meek as Moses."* A few weeks later, her husband beat William Howard Taft in the popular vote but lost to a former university professor named Woodrow Wilson.

Eventually all four of her sons left to serve in World War I, a cause completely supported by her husband. Echoing Martha Washington's response to that fateful Second Continental Congress, Edith wrote: "They have all gone away from the house on the hill [Sagamore], but it is all quite right and best." She lost three of her four sons to war and outlived her indefatigable Teddy by nearly thirty years, but it was her own funeral plans that best revealed the true meekness of Edith Roosevelt. She requested the simplest coffin possible, asking, for instance, that if the church did not have a pall to please cover her with one of her own crepe shawls. She wanted nothing on the coffin except pink and blue flowers from her family. The processional hymn should be "The Son of God," with "Love Divine" for the recessional and Beethoven's Ninth Symphony for the anthem. Finally, she noted, "Do not take off my wedding ring, and please no embalming."[17]

Meekness is obedience, amiability, gentleness, and patience. It is the effort to claim happiness and vitality from the hope of progress. It is a balance of dignity and long-suffering. In exchange, Christ's promise to the meek is a grand inheritance and a full heritage: That spiritual security which the world withheld God presents with great joy and unbridled affection and the promise that no one else can steal it.

Echoes of This Beatitude in the Bible

Psalm 37:29: "The righteous will inherit the land and dwell in it forever."

Galatians 5:23: "Gentleness and self-control. Against such things there is no law."

Galatians 6:1: "Brothers, if someone is caught in a sin, you who are spiritual should restore him gently. But watch yourself, or you also may be tempted."

Ephesians 4:2: "Be completely humble and gentle; be patient, bearing with one another in love."

James 1:21: "Therefore, get rid of all moral filth and the evil that is so prevalent, and humbly accept the word planted in you, which can save you."

Matthew 11:29: "Take my yoke upon you, and learn from me; for I am gentle and humble in heart, and you will find rest unto your souls."

First Lady Quotables

"I think the petition in the Litany, 'Strengthen those who stand, comfort the weak-hearted, raise up those who fall, and finally beat down Satan under our feet' is especially for boys going out into the big world. I have added it to my prayers."

—Edith Roosevelt, reflecting on the lives of her four sons

"I have been wonderfully blessed in the discretion of my wife. She is one of the coolest and best balanced women I ever saw. She is unstampedable. There has not been one solitary instance of my public career when I suffered in the smallest degree for any remark she ever made . . . many times such discretion has been a real blessing."

—James Garfield

"Daily I am impressed anew with the responsibility and opportunity which has been given me. In no sense does it overwhelm me, rather does it inspire me and increase my energy and I am so filled with the desire to measure up. . . ."

—Grace Coolidge

"Why is it so very rare in a man and woman to be simply intimate friends? Such a friendship is infinitely higher than what is usually called love, for in it there is a realization of each other's defects, and a proper appreciation of their good points without that fatal idealization which is so blind and, to me, so contemptible. . . . From my point of view a love which is worthy of the name should always have a beginning in the other. To have a man love you in any other way is no compliment."

—Helen Taft in her diary the fall of 1880

Photo on page 78:

Lady Bird Johnson walks quietly past a group of young people protesting the Vietnam War in Washington, D.C.

UPI/Bettmann

Blessed are those who hunger and thirst for righteousness, for they will be filled.

Hillary Clinton

Chapter Four

Blessed are those who hunger and thirst for righteousness, for they will be filled.

First Ladies As Social Reformers

Since the days of Martha Washington, our First Ladies have been a significant touchstone for our nation's morals and personal faith. The role of reformer and "guardian of the least among these" has often fallen into women's capable hands, and this almost always happened in the name of Christ and with plans developed in the church. In fact, this role, according to Edith Mayo, curator emeritus of the First Ladies Exhibit at the Smithsonian Institution in Washington, D.C., "is actually following a long and very honored tradition of women's activities in the community, in other words, extending the nurturing, if you will, beyond the home and into the larger home which is the community or the nation. That was a very esteemed role that women played all through the nineteenth century and it almost always grew out of religious motivations."

With its emphasis on righteousness, this Beatitude reflects the greatest contribution our First Ladies have made to social reform in America. Hunger and thirst reflect *intensity.* This is not just a craving. This is not an interest in experimenting with a new recipe for dinner. This isn't just a growling stomach. This is a "Listen to me: I haven't eaten in three days, and I'm going to do something about it" response that verges on obsession. Throughout Hebrew scripture as well as the New Testament, righteousness is linked to personal action, integrity, and vigilance. It is *not* noblesse oblige. This is *not* just a nice thing to do if you find the time. This Beatitude reflects bulldog tenacity, and if the legacy of the First Ladies' sense of righteousness could speak to America, it would say:

We stand for the marginalized, believing in the equality of all people.

We will make a difference for future generations.

Decisions are based on the answers to two simple questions: What is the greatest need I see? What is the best use of *my* talents?

An Important Word About Diversity

In light of these three standards, our First Ladies have responded with such remarkable diversity, it is essential to understand their varying religious perspectives to appreciate their individual contributions. The best recent example is the 1996 presidential campaign, which demonstrated that the difference between First Lady Hillary Clinton and First Lady hopeful Elizabeth Dole wasn't just Yale versus Harvard, liberal against conservative, Democrat opposing Republican. It was also social gospel versus evangelicalism, two unique positions within American Protestantism that each respond to the fourth Beatitude—and many other scriptural points—in distinctly different ways.

In fact, the religious contrast between these two women is a spiritual paradox that says as much about the current nature of American Protestantism as it does about the irony that one denomination could produce two deeply religious yet so diverse women as Mrs. Clinton and Mrs. Dole. Not since the 1976 presidential campaign involving moderate Southern Baptist Rosalynn Carter and Episcopalian Betty Ford had America heard prospective First Ladies speak so openly about their religious convictions. But unlike Rosalynn and Betty, Hillary and Elizabeth grew up in the same denomination. Both are products of devout Methodism. From the broader perspective of Protestantism, each woman is actually an icon, that is, each one represents religious ideals, beliefs, and characteristics shared by literally millions of other Americans.

Hillary Clinton is *social gospel,* a dangerously oversimplified term that gets interpreted along a continuum ranging from "meddling do-gooder" to "bonafide social reformer." Social gospel types promote the inevitable (some would say all-consuming) relationship between personal faith and social action. Reformers are inevitably controversial, and reformers who speak about the link between personal faith and a determination to change society often become the targets of religious conservatives. Recall the reaction to Martin Luther King, Jr., in his civil rights campaign and Jimmy Carter in his work toward peace and human rights, especially his trips to North Korea and Haiti in 1994. Politically, defenders of the social gospel concept are typically associated with Democrats, African Americans, and other minority groups such as Jews and Latinos.

Elizabeth Dole represents *evangelicalism,* a dangerously oversimplified term often linked to fundamentalism and one that gets interpreted along a completely different continuum. This one ranges from "out to lunch on society's real needs" to "genuine preserver of social values." Evangelicals are dedicated to holding firm to a core set of beliefs they feel should be preserved and defended—beliefs about the nature of Christ, the Bible, and traditional or shared community values.

Starting in 1987, Elizabeth Dole began talking to audiences about her own spiritual awakening, a gesture reminiscent of Jimmy Carter's openness on the presidential campaign trail in 1975. Now, of course Elizabeth Dole is interested and active in community, state, and national improvements. Of course Hillary Clinton can speak articulately about how her faith has influenced her personally. But it is the *degree* of expression that matters, especially as evidenced by personal behavior. Elizabeth Dole is out there talking about her born-again experience. Hillary Clinton is reforming segments of the population by overhauling Arkansas schools, claiming unprecedented tenure in the field of child advocacy, and attempting health care reform. This is not to suggest that one woman is responding to the fourth

Beatitude more appropriately than the other. It is, however, evidence that two women strongly dedicated to Christ's teachings can easily interpret those teachings differently and express their faith distinctively.

While some observers consider Hillary and Elizabeth's religious diversity a tribute to Methodism's tolerance of varied religious views and expressions of faith, others scratch their heads, wondering just how it could happen. In truth, Methodism does not hold the exclusive contract on producing spiritual diversity among its members. The Roman Catholic, Presbyterian, Episcopal, Lutheran, and United Church of Christ denominations all make room for diversity of beliefs among their followers, while Southern Baptists and independent evangelical denominations are likely to produce more homogenous and conservative political activists.

The contrast between these two women may also speak volumes about the relationship between the laity and the leaders of America's mainline Protestant churches and how each of those groups may respond to the fourth Beatitude. Those in denominational hierarchies who tend to be more liberal, open-minded, and pluralistic are likely to be drawn to Mrs. Clinton. People in the pew, however, who tend to be more conservative and, frankly, aren't so certain the church should be meddling in overhauling society anyway, are likely to prefer Mrs. Dole. They are also likely to find private, nongovernmental social programs to support.

Religion historian Dr. Martin Marty identifies three primary admonitions in the teachings of Methodist founder John Wesley which are foundational points for American Protestantism today and shed light on the unique paths of Mrs. Clinton and Mrs. Dole:

A Warmed, Changed Heart.

Wesley stood in great contrast to the staid and proper Church of England of his own background when he preached the need for personal conversion. He was certain, in fact, that by being born again, a person could develop the strength and grace essential to serve both Christ and the world. Elizabeth Dole is squarely defined by this element.

TRANSFORM THE WORLD.

This is the social gospel concept represented by Hillary Clinton, who early and often in her predominantly public life has quoted Wesley in his ferociously Type A predilection toward absolutes: "Do all the good you can, by all the means you can, in all the ways you can, in all the places you can, and all the times you can, to all the people you can, as long as ever you can."

For their differences, Hillary and Elizabeth share some important similarities that are essential to effectively responding to the fourth Beatitude. Both are well read in scripture, articulate about grappling with spiritual gray areas, and both are clearly products of a denomination that has historically emphasized education, public service, accountability of action, and a work ethic that has left both women described by the press as "an overachiever's overachiever." (An expression, incidentally, which also applied to Wesley.) "Paradox" is the first and last modifier to describe human spirituality. While Hillary and Elizabeth represent the yin and yang of Protestantism, both women are also perfect examples of what Marty described as Wesley's third foundational admonition:

ORGANIZE.

Organize your communities. Organize a church and then organize within that church. Create networks of support. Create networks that improve your community. This concept made Methodism extremely effective on the American frontier and also made it the largest denomination in the country for the first half of this century. It also is key to understanding how both Hillary and Elizabeth have been able to act on the fourth Beatitude with great effectiveness.

No matter their denominational backgrounds, no matter whether they are considered liberal or conservative politically, First Ladies have responded in the spirit of the fourth Beatitude since the founding of America, and "Children First" has been their most common theme. While their projects have varied, their causes typically land in one of three areas: education, health care, and personal safety of children. For the last two centuries First Ladies have intervened when children were orphaned by war or deadly epidemics like cholera and smallpox. They also fought against poor education, poverty, child labor, and inadequate medical care.

Several First Ladies, including Carrie Harrison and Lucretia Garfield, were teachers. Nellie Herron taught school for three years at a preparatory school for girls in Cincinnati before she married William Howard Taft in June 1886. Betty Ford taught dance to underprivileged children in Grand Rapids, and Ellen Wilson taught African American children in a mission over a saloon in New York City. Pat Nixon taught at Whittier Union High School, where she got a reputation as an advocate of disadvantaged Mexican American students. Unfairly called "Plastic Pat" in the White House because of her reserved nature, Richard Nixon's wife became animated when children entered the Executive Mansion, and once took a boy all the way to the private third floor quarters when he asked to see her washing machine.

Hillary Clinton

No First Lady in American history has been so dedicated to children and so controversial at the same time as Hillary Clinton. Her determination to contribute to the cause of child advocacy in education, health care, and the legal system was actually born from her Methodist upbringing. "Methodism has been important to me for as long as I can remember," she has often told reporters. "My father came from a long line of Methodists who had immigrated from England and Wales, and they took their church very seriously." When she and her brothers were born, even though they lived in Illinois, their parents took them back to Scranton, Pennsylvania, to be christened in front of her grandfather and other relatives at Court Street United Methodist, where her father had been baptized.

The First United Methodist Church in Park Ridge, Illinois, was large and active. She not only attended Sunday school and Sunday morning worship, she also went to Sunday evening youth group and often midweek activities as well. "The church was a critical part of my growing up. I almost couldn't even list all the ways it influenced me and helped me develop as a person, not only on my own faith journey but with a sense of obligations to others."

Confirmed in 1959 at the age of eleven, Hillary is a fascinating product of her denomination and its emphasis on linking faith to community action and defense of "the least among these." Her intelligence, energy, and financially comfortable environment in an upper-middle-class, strongly Republican suburb located just outside Chicago placed her in a well-protected environment that could have ridden out the threat of communism, the political assassinations of the 1960s, even the civil rights and women's movement with relative ease. She could have done this even while dedicating herself to God, country, and family, but Hillary Diane Rodham was influenced by a youth pastor who pounded away relentlessly at the lesson that a Christian *always* has an obligation to serve others. "[Rev. Don] Jones had been one of the key influences in Hillary Diane Rodham's life," wrote Donnie Radcliffe, "showing her and her friends that for many youngsters their age there was a world of despair and deprivation beyond the manicured lawns and backyard swings of Park Ridge."[1]

Jones introduced her to the writings of theologian Dietrich Bonhoeffer, a Lutheran pastor who was hanged in a Nazi prison camp April 1945 for his part in the Resistance. Bonhoeffer insisted the role of a Christian demanded total engagement in the world, promoting human development and emphasizing morality. She also met the mind of Reinhold Niebuhr, whose writings demonstrated the constant tension between pessimism regarding human nature and an intense passion for justice and human dignity. Heady stuff even for seminarians and experienced pastors, Hillary was reading this in high school and college.

"As I grew and studied on my own, I found the approach of Methodism to appeal to me and to be very compatible to my life," she said in 1992 during an interview with the United Methodist News Service. "On my first personal faith journey and my social commitments, the emphasis on personal salvation and active, applied Christianity . . . the practical method of trying to live as a Christian in a difficult, challenging world was very appealing to me."

In 1960, when she was thirteen, Hillary joined a baby-sitting group through her church, a group that looked after the children of migrant farm workers—Latinos and blacks who harvested crops on labor-intensive truck farms south and west of Park Ridge. Jones also combined his youth group with ghetto kids of the same age to discuss faith and personal experiences.

"We discussed what our faith meant in the world," Hillary said of her overall experience with her youth group, "and I am so grateful for those lessons and those opportunities."

When she was fifteen, Hillary went with Jones and the youth group into Chicago on April 15, 1962, to hear a speech by Rev. Martin Luther King, Jr. She was one of 2,500 who packed Orchestra Hall to hear the speech, appropriately titled "Remaining Awake Through a Revolution" and met King afterward, an event that was significant in its impact on her. While attending Wellesley College and then Yale Law School, she cemented her concerns and took a path that squarely established her in the field of child advocacy:

While a law student at Yale, Hillary explored her own interest in children's issues by interning for Marian Wright Edelman, another graduate of the school, who would go on to create the Children's Defense Fund. Through her link to Edelman, Hillary worked for then Senator Walter Mondale and his subcommittee, studying the use of migratory labor in America. She realized not just the defenselessness of children but the tragedy of children growing up in absolute poverty.

Hillary completed special studies through the Yale Child Study Center, where she learned about the medical, psychological, and developmental issues influencing children's lives. She also assisted the Yale New Haven Hospital create policies to deal with child abuse. At the same time, she traveled to Washington often to monitor hearings on Capitol Hill that applied to children's issues. Immediately after graduation, Hillary became staff attorney for the Children's Defense Fund.

After she married Bill Clinton in the fall of 1975, Hillary took her developing reputation as a child legal advocate to Arkansas, where her husband was elected to the post of state attorney general the following year. Both were ardent campaigners for Jimmy Carter in the 1976 election, and Carter in late 1977 appointed Hillary to a two-year term on the Legal Services Corporation, a federally funded, not-for-profit program providing legal assistance to the poor.

When her husband became governor of Arkansas in 1978, Hillary began an impressive list of achievements for that state. She founded the Arkansas Advocates for Children and Families, was chairman of the Governor's Rural Health Advisory Committee, continued her work on the Legal Services Corporation, and became a board member of the Children's Defense Fund. In early 1983 she became her husband's choice to head his task force to overhaul the antiquated Arkansas educational system and bring it out of the basement regarding national ranking. She and her committee members traveled the state for several months, studying students' greatest needs, touring broken-down buildings, talking to parents and administrators, and forming an extensive, thorough plan that involved improving facilities, capping classroom size, slightly lengthening the school year, and—the most controversial of all—calling for teachers' proficiency exams.

Hillary also brought to Arkansas a program called Home Instruction Program for Preschool Youngsters (HIPPY), which won the attention and congratulations of then First Lady Barbara Bush, an advocate of literacy.

In 1995 she published the book *It Takes a Village: And Other Lessons Children Teach Us.* In it she quotes government statistics regarding America's youth today: One in five lives in poverty; ten million children do not have private or public health care coverage; nearly 7,000 children die every year from suicide or homicide; one in four of all children born in America is born to an unmarried mother; and 135,000 children bring guns to school each day. "Everywhere we look, children are under assault: from violence and neglect, from the breakup of families, from the temptations of alcohol, tobacco, sex, and drug abuse, from greed, materialism, and spiritual emptiness," she wrote in *It Takes a Village.*

Throughout her speeches and other writings, Hillary has effectively linked her faith to her actions:

> I am particularly indebted to the many people who taught Sunday school and vacation Bible school. I can remember the lessons there, sometimes more vividly than what I have read or seen just last week. How many times did I sing the song, "Jesus Loves the Little Children of the World." "Red and yellow, black and white/They are precious in His sight." Those words have stayed with me more personally and longer than many earnest lectures on race relations. And to this day, I find myself wondering how anyone who ever sang them could be prejudiced against any group.[2]

Here, in the United States . . . we see too many children and people who remain on the margins of society. We see children who are unloved, unfed, unhealthy, and unschooled. We see women and people of color who are marginalized because they are denied the opportunities they deserve to become full participants in society, those who are the continuing challenges. And yet, we now know much more about what we can do together to meet those challenges. Despite the problems of poverty and illiteracy and violence, there are solutions being born, being born in churches and communities throughout the world.[3]

In my book, I wrote a little chapter called Children Are Born Believers because I feel so strongly that we owe our children a chance for them to have a spiritual life. For them to be part of a church, and it is not only something we do for them. We do it for ourselves, and we know that in ways we might not even predict consequences can be positive. A recent survey of young people and drug use found that children and youth who had regular religious involvement and attendance in a church or synagogue were far less likely to engage in self-destructive behavior like drug use. So we do it because we believe and we do it because we trust that it will lead our young people to a better life for themselves.[4]

Preaching is a distant second to practicing when it comes to instilling values like compassion, courage, faith, fellowship, forgiveness, love, peace, hope, wisdom, prayer, and humility. By putting spiritual values in action, adults show children that they are not just for church or home but are to be brought into the world, used to make the village a better place.[5]

Then we should be asking ourselves, "What areas of common agreement do we have that can lead us as individuals, as a church, as a community and society to work together on behalf of our children?" We know the biblical admonitions about caring for each other. We know so well what Jesus said to his disciples in Mark, holding a small child in his arms that 'Whoever welcomes one such child in my name, welcomes me, and whoever welcomes me, welcomes not me but the one who sends me.' If we could only keep that in mind, and see in every child's face that faithful, hopefulness.[6]

Righteous First Ladies

Dolley Madison regularly visited the poor in Washington and was interested in promoting literacy as well. However, it was the Washington City Orphans' Asylum that became the first official project of any First Lady. In October 1815 she coordinated a meeting to raise money and resources for the cause. She herself donated $20 and a cow. Dolley became the first director of the organization charged with building the asylum. She sewed clothes for the children, made friends with women of all social classes, urging them to sew as well, and eventually the children's home was built just one block from the White House.

Former First Lady Abigail Adams enrolled one of her two black servants in the local schools, and when a townsman objected, saying the white students would quit school, she said:

> The Boy is a Freeman as much as any of the Young Men, and merely because his Face is Black, is he to be denied instruction, how is he to be qualified to procure a livelihood? Is this the Christian principle of doing to others as we would have others do to us? . . . I have not thought it any disgrace to my self to take him into my parlour and teach him both to read and write. . . . I hope we shall go to Heaven together.[7]

When she was first lady of California, Nancy Reagan endorsed the Foster Grandparent Program, an organization encouraging relationships between children and senior citizens. In the fall of 1981 she helped write *To Love a Child,* which included accounts of some youth and elderly who participated in the program. She also arranged for book profits to go to the Foster Grandparent Program. Her best known contribution to children, however, was her tireless dedication to fighting drug abuse among America's youth.

She traveled the country speaking on the subject, attended antidrug conferences, met with children and parents' groups and visited drug rehabilitation centers. She even appeared in a cameo role for one episode of *Diff'rent Strokes,* in which she discouraged drug use.

When one child asked her, "What should I say if someone offers me drugs?" she responded, "Just say no." This public exchange resulted in the grass-roots creation of Just Say No clubs throughout the United States.

Lady Bird Johnson endorsed Head Start, a federally funded program designed to help preschoolers from disadvantaged families in early childhood development and preparation for school. Rachel Jackson and Hannah Van Buren were known for their charity toward the poorest children in their communities.

Abigail Fillmore promoted literacy during her years in the White House. Barbara Bush *is* the First Lady of Literacy, however, because her dedication to the cause has spanned decades. She often explained to audiences the devastating ripple effects of illiteracy, including drug use, poverty, unwanted pregnancy, crime, poor health habits, and voter and civic apathy. Because of Barbara's focus on the problem when she lived in the White House, America learned just how far illiteracy extended: About thirty-five million American adults couldn't read above the eighth-grade level. Nearly twenty-three million were functionally illiterate, meaning they were not performing above a fourth-grade reading and writing level. She also helped create the Barbara Bush Foundation for Family Literacy with an initial $1 million in private funds.

Through the Carter Center in Atlanta, Rosalynn Carter maintains a full schedule in continued dedication to the mentally ill, the mentally retarded, and to several programs aimed at improving the health of the world's children. The Carter Center works closely with the Task Force for Child Survival and Development, which was formed in 1984 to coordinate and expand global immunization efforts. Working with its major sponsors—the Rockefeller Foundation, the World Health Organization, UNICEF, the World Bank, and the United Nations Development Program—the task force successfully raised the immunization rate of the world's children from twenty to eighty percent in just six years.

The task force then expanded its goals to achieve the following by the year 2000: the global eradication of polio, a ninety-percent reduction in measles cases and a ninety-five-percent reduction in deaths from measles, a fifty-percent drop in maternal mortality rates. In addition, the Carter Center and the task force created in 1992 a program titled All Kids Count, which promotes tracking childhood immunizations.

In 1991 Rosalynn joined forces with Betty Bumpers, the wife of United States Senator Dale Bumpers, to create Every Child by Two, which emphasizes the importance of early immunization. The program seeks to educate parents, promote long-term policy changes to ensure vaccination for all United States children by age two, and encourages health departments to expand access to immunization services. This program is now established in about forty states, and more than seventy national organizations have become partners in the immunization campaign.

When she was nineteen, Eleanor Roosevelt taught classes at the Rivington Street Settlement House on Manhattan's Lower East Side. She gave lessons in dance and exercise to the daughters of Jewish and Italian immigrants. "The dirty streets, crowded with foreign-looking people, filled me with terror . . . but the children interested me enormously," she wrote. "I still remember the glow of pride that ran through me when one of the little girls said her father wanted me to come home with her, as he wanted to give me something because she enjoyed her classes so much."

As a representative of the Junior League, an organization of wealthy young society women who served the underprivileged, she also was asked that year to inspect factories and department stores employing young female workers. After touring several sweatshops, Eleanor wrote: "I was appalled. . . . I was frightened to death. But this is what had been required of me and I wanted to be useful. I entered my first sweatshop and walked up the steps of my first tenement. . . . I saw little children of four or five sitting at [work] tables until they dropped with fatigue."[8]

Eleanor remained dedicated to children throughout her life, and in the fall of 1962, as her seventy-eighth birthday approached and she knew she faced her own death in a matter of weeks, she gave orders that she wanted lots of little children at her party. On October 11 she celebrated with some friends and their children and grandchildren. On November 7 she died of a stroke, brought on by complications of an untreatable blood disease.

But not all First Ladies have gushed over maternal interests or obligations.

A college graduate and an expert in both Latin and Greek, Lucretia Garfield felt a great responsibility and affection to her own children but also maintained a well-documented sense of detachment. In a letter to her husband dated June 5, 1877, and surely intended to be kept private, the intelligent, articulate, and deeply religious woman ironically known as "Discreet Crete" revealed outright resentment for her traditional responsibilities.

"It is horrible to be a man, but the grinding misery of being a woman between the upper and nether millstone of household cares and training children is almost as bad," she wrote to her husband. "To be half civilized with some aspirations for enlightenment and obliged to spend the largest part of the time the victim of young barbarians keeps one in perpetual ferment."[9]

Lou Hoover

Before Rwanda, before Bosnia, before the Marshall Plan, there was Belgium, invaded without warning in the opening days of the First World War. The Belgian government fought to hold a small strip of its own territory between France and Germany. Most civilians, however, were caught inside territory controlled by the German Army of Occupation, which did not consider feeding enemy civilians a high strategic priority. The greatest threat to the Belgians was not death by German technological warfare but death by starvation. Before live CNN coverage of the Gulf War, before a stunned America watched police turn fire hoses and angry dogs against black activists (a sight that helped pass civil rights legislation in the 1960s), there was a quiet, desperate virtually invisible populace in a tiny European country facing mass annihilation.

In 1914 there was a relatively small number of Americans and Europeans standing between the common people of Belgium and literal starvation. Lou Hoover was one of those people, and she was nothing less than ferocious in her determination and efforts. World War I ushered in several new horrors of war, but along with mustard gas and the tank came another innovation—the international humanitarian relief program. Along with her husband, Lou was a major player in this first worldwide effort.

Not only did she volunteer at the Belgian Relief headquarters in London, she also visited Belgium directly to see firsthand the desperate situation. She traveled the United States, making speeches to raise money and supplies for the cause and even persuaded the Rockefeller Foundation to provide free shipping of American food and clothing to Belgium. One of the most touching footnotes to this story is that America literally sent thousands of fifty-pound bags of flour into Belgium, and the people of that country were so poor that to express their thanks, they transformed some of the huge cloth bags into embroidered artwork and then presented those to relief officials. During the dreadful years of 1914 and 1915, the contents of these sacks kept the civilian population of Belgium alive. For the impoverished Belgians, embroidering the flour sacks was their only way to thank the relief workers, who, incidentally, were often so cherished by the Belgians, their popularity was typically second only to the Belgian royal family. When King Leopold presented her with the Cross Chevalier, Order of Leopold, Lou Hoover commented simply, "What is there to say? I have done nothing extraordinary. . . ."

But for the millions of Belgians who, because of her intervention, survived the most desperate circumstances faced by any human, and for those of us who are inspired into action by her example, Lou Hoover's work in Europe at the outbreak of World War I was, indeed, extraordinary.

Grace Coolidge

"As a fellow trustee of Clarke School for the Deaf in Northampton I have a strong personal recollection of her untiring devotion and labors throughout her life to this most worthy cause," wrote United States Senator John Kennedy. "Since her days in the White House she continued to epitomize the qualities of graciousness, charm, and modesty which marked her as an ideal First Lady of the Land."[10] He spoke of Grace Coolidge.

Grace Goodhue had an upbringing similar to other First Ladies. She grew up an active member of her Protestant church. When she attended the University of Vermont, she joined the College Street Congregational Church, where she sang in the choir and attended services as well as Bible studies and Christian Endeavor meetings. Grace graduated from the university in 1902 and accepted a teaching position at the Clarke Institute for the Deaf in Northampton. She taught first in the primary grades and then in the intermediate school. Grace taught for three years before she married Calvin Coolidge, and while marriage always signaled the end of a woman's career in the early years of the twentieth century, Grace's dedication to this cause continued until her own death in the 1950s.

Unlike most First Ladies of her century, Grace did not use the bully pulpit that came with her position. She did, however, in a consistent, gentle way raise support, awareness, and money for the Clarke school. She had a wide smile, beautiful eyes, and a friendly manner that clearly contrasted her socially awkward, tight-lipped husband. In the years that stretched between their wedding, her husband's service as both the lieutenant governor and then governor of Massachusetts, and his selection as Warren Harding's vice president, Grace was removed from the public eye. She was a wife, and a mother to their two boys. She was an active member of the Edwards Congregational Church in Northampton, sewing for the church's women's guild and attending the church suppers and bazaars.

When Calvin Coolidge received the news that Warren Harding died, Grace took on the role of First Lady with relative ease. In the White House she was a gracious hostess and often served as an effective bridge between her stiff husband and his political colleagues. With her softness, gentility, and charm, she was nearly the exact opposite of the woman she replaced, Florence Harding.

As First Lady she invited many famous deaf people to the White House, including Helen Keller. Grace permanently endeared herself to former president and then Chief Justice William Howard Taft by seeking out and conversing with his half brother, Charles, and his wife, Annie, who were both deaf. Grace also sparked a $2 million drive for the Clarke school while she was in the White House. In fact, during his speech as outgoing president, Calvin Coolidge thanked Americans for supporting the cause that meant so much to his wife.

In the final years of her life she touched off a centennial development program for the school, a program which would reach fruition in 1967, ten years after her death. Grace's progressive views about the handicapped strongly influenced her husband as well. At the time of his own death,

Calvin Coolidge was working with Helen Keller on a special project for the blind. In her last years, with handwriting wavering from ill health, Grace sent letters to a young Henry Cabot Lodge and to many other well-known figures, asking them to serve on the Clarke school's national committee of sponsors, but she also wanted them to educate the general public about the enormous problems that face a deaf child. Helen Keller, Spencer Tracy, and Herbert Hoover, Jr., were among those who participated.

Grace especially looked forward to the day when deaf children might enjoy the same educational opportunities as the hearing, and she was thrilled to watch the school's graduates share in team sports, go to college, learn to drive cars, and land fulfilling employment in the real world.

Even in her final years she was dedicated to her church in traditional ways—bake sales, potluck socials, and funding drives. She died July 8, 1957, and the next day the *New York Times* observed:

> Warm, outgoing, understanding . . . Grace Goodhue Coolidge was in many respects of personality the antithesis of her husband; but in one important respect they were alike. They were both unpretentious, unaffected children of the New England soil. . . . Mrs. Coolidge's death yesterday cannot help but recall a glittering era in American history, the "Golden Twenties"; but her qualities of mind and heart represented something far deeper and more lasting in American life.[11]

In 1939 she raised funds to bring child refugees from Germany into the United States. In 1940 she helped raise money for the Queen Wilhelmina Fund for the Dutch victims of the Nazi invaders. After the bombing of Pearl Harbor, she volunteered for the Red Cross, civil defense programs, and wartime conservation drives. But her greatest contribution was her dedication to America's deaf citizens, and she made certain their cause was heard throughout the country.

Inspiring as these stories may be for us, as effective as they are in demonstrating what we humans can do when we take action in the spirit of the fourth Beatitude, they are meant to be balanced with the broader foundation of scripture. They are meant to be read and studied and internalized. You and I may be as different as the social gospel of Hillary Clinton and the evangelicalism of Elizabeth Dole, but the link between faith and action is one of the most prominent themes of scripture. It also is the driving force that has produced some of the most remarkable achievements of our First Ladies—and us common folks too.

Echoes of This Beatitude in the Bible

Matthew 6:33: "But seek first his kingdom and his righteousness, and all these things will be given to you as well."

Romans 6:18: "You have been set free from sin and have become slaves to righteousness."

Romans 14:17–18: "For the kingdom of God is not a matter of eating and drinking, but of righteousness, peace and joy in the Holy Spirit, because anyone who serves Christ in this way is pleasing to God and approved by men."

I Timothy 6:11: "But you, man of God, flee from all this, and pursue righteousness, godliness, faith, love, endurance and gentleness."

Hebrews 1:9: "You have loved righteousness and hated wickedness; therefore God, your God, has set you above your companions by anointing you with the oil of joy."

James 3:18: "Peacemakers who sow in peace raise a harvest of righteousness."

Psalm 23:3 "He restores my soul. He guides me in paths of righteousness for his name's sake."

Psalm 97:6 "The heavens proclaim his righteousness, and all the peoples see his glory."

Psalm 103:17–18 "But from everlasting to everlasting the Lord's love is with those who fear him, and his righteousness with their children's children—with those who keep his covenant and remember to obey his precepts."

II Timothy 4:7–8: "I have fought the good fight, I have finished the race, I have kept the faith. Now there is in store for me the crown of righteousness which the Lord, the righteous Judge, will award to me on that day. . . ."

Psalm 17:15 "And I—in righteousness I will see your face; when I awake, I will be satisfied with seeing your likeness."

First Lady Quotables

"We must not just accept things that are wrong and placidly sit back and say, 'Well, people have stood that for a long while, they'll probably live through it some time longer,' and be content with things as they are. You've got to want to change the things that are not satisfactory. You have got to want to do it so much that you will take some trouble about it."

—Eleanor Roosevelt

"I wish more churches—and parents—took seriously the teachings of every major religion that we treat one another as each of us would want to be treated. If that happened, we could make significant inroads on the social problems we confront. . . . Religion is not just about one's relationship with God, but about what values flow out of that relationship, how we follow them in our daily lives and especially in our treatment of our neighbors next door and all over the world."

—Hillary Clinton

"A few days ago there appeared in the paper a story of a manager in an airport restaurant in Houston, Texas, who had mistaken the Indian Ambassador and his companion for Negroes and had requested them to move from the regular restaurant to a small room reserved for Negroes. . . . Every person I have met almost since this came out in the papers has spoken to me of it with indignation, surprise and horror. How could an ambassador be treated in this way? A better question is: How could any human being be treated in this way?"

—Eleanor Roosevelt, *My Day*, September 2, 1955

Photo on page 100:

Hillary Clinton campaigns for health care reform and child advocacy during an educational fair on childhood health issues.

Reuters/Bettmann

Blessed are the merciful, for they will be shown mercy.

Pat Nixon

Chapter Five

Blessed are the merciful,

for they will be shown mercy.

The Merciful First Ladies

The fifth Beatitude is probably the easiest to define because of mercy's inevitable link to simplicity. Mercy doesn't ask a lot of questions, and it usually doesn't even ask, "Does this person deserve assistance?" It simply acts—and, in doing so, is a faith statement that says even more about the giver than the receiver.

Mercy is linked to justice, grace, and human dignity. It is a deliberate act that begins with empathy, develops as the giver concludes she can and must contribute *something* to the situation, and ends with action itself. For First Ladies, it may be as easy as helping a stranger who sends a note to the White House for assistance or as dangerous as Pat Nixon's trip to Peru in 1970 after an earthquake killed more than 65,000 there.

Ellen Wilson

On the morning of August 6, 1914, Ellen Wilson lay dying in her bedroom in the White House. An anxious president hovered over her, and their close friend and physician, Cary Grayson, monitored her final hours. What followed was a poignant, bittersweet moment that demonstrated Ellen Wilson died the way she had lived: "I would go more peacefully," she is said to have whispered, "if my bill would pass."

Her bill was legislation designed to improve the plight of thousands of Washington's poorest citizens. Word was sent to Capitol Hill: "She is dying. She wants this done." Word went back to the White House: "It will be passed without haste and without question."

From the start of her husband's term in office in 1913, Ellen Wilson presided over the White House with grace and charm and unobtrusive efficiency. She had managed her father's parsonage after her mother's death. When her husband served as president of Princeton University, and then governor of New Jersey, their home often overflowed with guests and members of their own extended families who needed special attention. For Ellen Wilson the role of social hostess came as second nature.

It was Ellen's role as social *worker* and her hopes to improve housing for thousands of Washington's poorest citizens that earned her the title Angel in the White House. Some historians refer to her as the "first First Lady with a real cause," and though this seems unfair to earlier presidents' wives, her example of mercy was profound.

Ellen Wilson's special concern became the back alleys of Washington, where thousands of families—mostly African American—lived in primitive destitution. Some of them lived within blocks of the Capitol yet remained largely concealed from the most prosperous residents and influential policy makers. Shortly after her husband's inauguration, Ellen met with Charlotte Hopkins, chairperson of a Washington chapter of the National Civic Federation, and they discussed the dwellings, some of which were converted stables, hastily built from cheap material to house poor black workers. The slums were rat-infested firetraps with no plumbing and were clearly unfit for the thousands of people forced to live there. Just three days after her meeting with Mrs. Hopkins, she toured the worst slums but without disclosing her identity.

Stunned by what she saw, Ellen used her influence and position to draw constant attention to their plight, giving tours to congressmen, becoming honorary chairperson of the NCF, and sitting on the board of an organization that raised money for housing improvements.

In her brief time as First Lady, she also championed the cause of female government workers when she began making unannounced visits to the poorly lit and unsafe workplaces like the Government Printing Office. Her interests also extended into truancy laws, child labor, and the care of the mentally ill. But it was her dedication to Washington's poorest—especially in the hour of her own death—that was the greatest gift of mercy given in the life of Ellen Axson Wilson.

Woodrow Wilson first met Ellen in April 1883, when he was in Rome, Georgia, tending to some legal matters for his mother. On Sunday morning, Wilson attended the local Presbyterian church, where he discovered both the pastor, who was a friend of his father's, and the pastor's daughter, who had "a bright, pretty face." Though Ellen wore a mourning veil, Woodrow sensed "that this demure little lady has lots of life and fun in her."[1]

Had he checked with the young men of Rome, Wilson might have been discouraged in the beginning, for it was common knowledge in the community that Ellen Axson had vowed never to marry because her family needed her. Her mother had died three years before, and her father was of uncertain mental stability. She was needed as surrogate to three younger children. But when he visited the parsonage that afternoon, Wilson decided to initiate a courtship that resulted in a marriage of remarkable tenderness and partnership and one that probably produced the most passionate set of love letters exchanged by any presidential couple.

They were married June 24, 1885, in the parsonage of the Independent Presbyterian Church of Savannah, Georgia. The bride's grandfather and the groom's father officiated the ceremony. The joy that marriage brought Ellen Wilson was not only well deserved, it may have saved her sanity. In addition to being a mother to her three younger siblings, Ellen had to deal with her father's ever more apparent mental illness. In early 1884 Edward Axson—in a state of violence—was committed to the Georgia State Mental Hospital, where he took his own life in May.

While her fiancé responded by wanting to get married as soon as possible, Ellen withdrew—apparently evaluating her family's tendency toward psychological breakdowns, which were taught and thought to be a result of spiritual or moral weakness. She did not have second thoughts about Woodrow as a husband. She did not have second thoughts about whether she loved him. She knew she did. Ellen Axson worried about inadvertently heaping upon him what had already been heaped upon her.

Woodrow assuaged her fears, and she discovered in marriage she could provide a stable environment not only to her siblings—who lived with her off and on—but to other relatives who needed her. In the early 1890s, while Wilson was a professor at Princeton, his sister and brother-in-law died within months of each other, leaving four children. In 1895 Wilson's sister Annie became widowed, and she and her daughter needed assistance as well. The home of Woodrow and Ellen Wilson was often considered a stable point in the difficult lives of their relatives.

Regarding the history of America's First Ladies, her death was especially tragic because unlike many who preceded her, Ellen Wilson demonstrated she knew the power of her bully pulpit. One can only imagine what else she might have achieved had she been granted more time.

In March 1914 Ellen took a bad fall in her bedroom and was then confined for several weeks. She did make a few public appearances after that, but by June, Dr. Grayson told her she suffered from Bright's disease as well as tuberculosis of the kidneys. There was simply no hope of recovery. She was listless and weak, and the president began spending hours by her bedside—urging her to eat, reading to her, praying for recovery, or watching her while she slept.

Trying also to cope with news that war seemed inevitable in Europe, an exasperated Wilson wrung his hands by her bed and said, "I can think of nothing—nothing, when my dear one is suffering."[2] He insisted that no one tell her of the conflict that loomed overseas.

On the morning of her death, August 6, 1914, Ellen expressed to her husband her last wish—that Congress pass the slum-clearance bill on which she'd worked so hard. Word reached the Senate floor and without further examination, without fully considering its total impact on Washington's poorest African American families, Congress passed "Mrs. Wilson's bill." (The flaw of the legislation is that it only cleared the slums. It did not fully address the issue of new housing for those black families.)

After her lifetime of dedication to her own desperate father and siblings, after all she'd attempted to do for Washington's poorest citizens, after her efforts to improve workplace conditions, Ellen's final act of mercy came just before her death—when she asked Dr. Grayson to look after Woodrow.

The funeral of Ellen Wilson was held in the East Room of the White House on August 10, 1914. The president and his immediate family accompanied the hearse to Union Station and then made the long, painful journey back to Rome, Georgia. The funeral train passed slowly through many Southern towns, where crowds gathered at the stations to honor the First Lady. Struck low by the paralyzing realization that a world can end, Wilson sat beside the coffin during most of the excruciating trip.

Once they reached Rome, a brief service was held in the same church where Wilson first saw his future wife. She was buried in a cemetery near the church and located not far from the Etowah River, where he first told her he loved her.

From the start of his life with Ellen, he was more outspoken about his feelings than she was. "I am so glad I am young so that I can give my youth to you," he once wrote to her. "I have found out now what it meant that I was once reserved, sensitive, morbid, almost cold. It meant that I had never begun to live." Beginning with their courtship, he delighted in the effect his warm affection had on her soul. "Think of the shy little maid who used to confess to hot blushes whenever she so much as wrote a single sentence of her heart's thoughts to me and who, found it hard . . . even to whisper, 'I love you.' " After they got married, he revealed remarkable candor regarding their intimate relationship. "You are the only pupil I ever have had or shall have in this delightful study of love-making." And at the very end, America's president sobbed uncontrollably when his wife's casket was lowered into the ground. "God has stricken me almost beyond what I can bear," he wrote to a friend.[3]

Eleanor Roosevelt

She was, by nature, an optimist, but First Lady Eleanor Roosevelt had an impressive capacity for staring down the unpleasant reality of human failings. With intelligence and determination she proved she was able to reach past those failings—whether in individuals or an entire culture—and bring human dignity back to the top of the list, where she felt it always belonged.

Her own acts of mercy during the White House years and beyond were vast—from befriending tramps to continuing Ellen Wilson's work in the Washington slums—but in the spirit of the fifth Beatitude, perhaps her greatest contribution came from her writing and its effectiveness at demonstrating the inevitable link between mercy, justice, and love, especially as those concepts were visible in the social fabric of America:

> "The one other thing [children] learn is that real love accepts people with their weaknesses as well as their strengths. You like to respect and admire someone whom you love, but actually you often love even more the people who require understanding and who make mistakes and have to grow with their mistakes." *(My Day,* March 27, 1958)

In the face of America's traditional and unfortunate anti-Semitic views, she wrote a column honoring the eleventh anniversary of the Warsaw ghetto uprising of Polish Jews against their Nazi captors in 1943 and paid tribute to the courage of the oppressed.

> This day has a meaning for all people everywhere because it proves that in the face of almost impossible difficulties men and women preferred certain death and fought together for the reputation and dignity of the individual human being. Warsaw was the center of Jewish spiritual and cultural life. . . . After conquering Poland, the Germans created the world's largest ghetto and set about exterminating all life within. . . . They treated all Jews with utter contempt, and the spiritual degradation that was forced upon them was more

humiliating, and in some ways more terrifying than the outright murder which they often found awaiting them in unexpected places. . . . In commemorating this great heroic action we commemorate not only the high spirit and the courage of these Jewish people, we commemorate and call to mind also the many instances in history when men and women in other areas of the world belonging to other nations, members of other races and of other religions, have also chosen death rather than humiliation and slow extermination. Human beings rise to great heights at certain times, and it is well to commemorate those heights and not to forget them, for they spur others to live with high standards and to dare greatly and to face even death with great fortitude." *(My Day,* April 22, 1954)

After watching the play *The Diary of Anne Frank,* Eleanor wrote:

As I left the theatre my heart was heavy, for I realized that people had actually lived through these scenes—and can we say with absolute assurance that they will never live through them again? I think we can say that the conscience of human beings was greatly awakened by what happened to people before and during World War II but was it enough to keep us from ever permitting ourselves or our neighbors to indulge in hate of our brother now? Do we understand, at last, that freedom must be universal and that all men must be assured that there will be respect for the individual human being, regardless of his race, his creed or his color? *(My Day,* October 15, 1955)

Those were the days when on a questionnaire I would put down "housewife" and feel very proud of it, and I am quite sure that no woman has any reason for feeling humiliated by the title. It is one of the most skilled professions in the world. When one adds to the business of running a house the care and bringing up of children, there is so much needed preparation for this occupation that I think it could be classed today among the most skilled occupations in the world. To be sure, there are good and bad homes; and there are children who are well brought up and children who are badly brought up. This happens in any business or professional activity. But when one adds up what it means to a nation, one must concede that the well-run home and the well-brought-up children are more important even than a well-run business. More people are affected by the occupation of a housewife and mother than are ever touched by any single business, no matter how large it may be. (*My Day,* October 17, 1955)

Southerners always bring up the question of marriage between the races, and I realize that that is the question of real concern to people. But it seems to me a very personal question which must be settled by family environment and by the development of the cultural and social patterns within a country. One can no longer lay down rules as to what individuals will do in any area of their lives in a world that is changing as fast as ours is changing today. (*My Day,* May 20, 1954)

In the Face of International Disaster

Betty Ford

When Betty Ford made a trip to Europe with her husband in late 1956 while he was a member of the United States House of Representatives, she found herself a witness to the Hungarian uprising that rocked that region throughout the fall and winter. As the Fords arrived in Vienna, Hungarians were flooding into Austria, and volunteers through the American embassy established a soup kitchen, where Betty helped serve hot stew.

She could not speak their language, she explained in her autobiography *The Times of My Life,* but she could tell by the strained looks on their faces what they were going through. The Fords toured some of the barracks where the Austrian authorities were housing refugees and discovered people were actually being billeted in an old German encampment left over from World War II, barracks with no working plumbing and no beds.

She was horrified when she discovered the refugees, even the babies, were sleeping on nothing but straw. Thinking of her own children, who were safe and happy back in the United States, she spent much of her time with the refugees, holding infants to keep them warm. So few of the Hungarians had adequate clothing, and there was no heat. "I wanted all these sad, tired people to have blankets and coats, to be protected against the night and the pain of loss, and there was nothing in the world I could do about it. . . . I felt useless, like a frivolous woman who's taken too much for granted."[4]

Pat Nixon

In June 1970—on a mission of mercy she herself initiated—First Lady Patricia Nixon flew to Lima, Peru, on *Air Force One.* Relief supplies loaded on the president's plane and one other air force jet weighed nine tons. On May 31, 1970, an earthquake under Huascaran Mountain in a remote part of the country killed at least 65,000 people and left another 800,000 homeless. The international community responded with aid, but Pat Nixon had become more distressed with each news update. Three weeks after the event, as she and the president quietly celebrated their thirtieth wedding anniversary at Camp David, Pat told her husband she wished she could do something to help.

He suggested she make a trip to Peru, and when she agreed he went to the phone immediately and made the arrangements. One great irony of her mercy trip to Peru is that in April 1958, when then–vice president and Mrs. Richard Nixon made a goodwill trip to that country, they faced open hostility initiated by Peruvian Communists, who pelted Mr. Nixon's car (Pat was not with him) and chanted "Death to Nixon" as he tried to enter San Marcos University to make a speech. At the Grand Hotel Bolivar where they stayed, Pat fell asleep to the nightmarish sound of an anti-Nixon, anti-American litany in the streets below. That had been a very difficult trip also, but, according to her daughter Julie, nothing was as bad as this one.

"Mother had visited combat hospitals, a leper colony, and the often impoverished institutions for the homeless," she wrote in *Pat Nixon: The Untold Story.* "But she had never encountered such utter misery. Her response was to hug the Peruvians who gathered around her." Her response to their tragedy, in fact, had positive political repercussions for the United States, because Peru then began to soften its long-standing anti-American, pro-Soviet stance. One Peruvian official said, "Her coming here meant more than anything else President Nixon could have done."

Rosalynn Carter

In the mid-1970s the world saw a drastic, tragic increase in refugees in Indochina, Africa, and Southeast Asia. In the fall of 1979 there was a new wave of displaced persons as Cambodians flooded into Thailand. In her autobiography *First Lady from Plains,* Rosalynn Carter explained that based on the huge number and poor condition of the refugees reaching Thailand, an entire race could be facing extinction. Through briefings with the State Department she learned that half the total population of Cambodia (also called Kampuchea) had died and that the Pol Pot government had exterminated more than one million of its own.

On November 9, 1978, she made a twenty-two-hour flight to Thailand and received briefings throughout the journey and warnings of what to expect. Nothing, however, prepared her for the human suffering she saw in the refugee camps when she arrived. In one camp she found literally acres of blue plastic makeshift tents held up by sticks. Inside were emaciated human beings of all ages, sick and dying from malnutrition and disease—Cambodians simply trying to get some relief from the heat, the flies, and the mosquitoes. With the odor of human waste all around her, she felt momentarily paralyzed and then took action that was both courageous and a natural part of her personality. Rosalynn fought back tears and reached out to touch some of the refugees.

Lying on the ground on dirty rags and mats, the refugees were in various stages of starvation or suffered malaria, dysentery, or tuberculosis. Seeing the children was the most difficult part of all, she said. Rosalynn stood in the middle of a large tent and held a baby girl who did not even have the strength to hold up her own arms. Rosalynn said she felt like a new mother again, thinking of her own four children, especially her daughter Amy. "How I loved her and what a joy she was, and what opportunities she had ahead of her! And what about this baby girl? What was ahead for her; what would her future be? Clutching her to me and looking at the poverty and disease and suffering around me, tears welled up in my eyes again. I thought of our country and how little we realize of the suffering and distress and grief in the world."[5]

As she left the camp she learned that the baby girl she had been holding died.

Rosalynn's involvement improved coordination between relief agencies, raised awareness by her presence and her public service spots, and helped raise $70 million—all of which brought permanent improvements to the lives of the Cambodians.

Elizabeth Monroe

James Monroe's wife might have gone down in history as the First Lady who never quite lived up to the expectations as a hostess for Washington society if not for her courageous act of mercy that occurred in France in 1794.

While her husband served as the American minister to France, Elizabeth became involved in efforts to free from prison Madame de Lafayette, wife of General Lafayette, who was a long-standing friend of the American government. During the Monroes' forty-five-day sea voyage from America to Paris, the French Revolution took a violent swing, and Robespierre had been executed just a week before they arrived.

Knowing that Madame de Lafayette was to face the guillotine, Elizabeth carried out a plan created by her husband. She rode to the prison in a carriage boldly displaying that it belonged to the American minister. In his notes on the encounter, Monroe wrote:

> As soon as one [carriage] could be procured & equipped for me, Mrs. Monroe drove in it to her prison door, and demanded an interview with Mdme. La Fayette. All eyes were fixed on the carriage & the inquiry general, to whom it belonged. To the American minister was the answer. Mdme. La Fayette was overwhelmed by the occurrence. She ran out precipitately and frantic to the iron railing of her prison gate, to greet her unknown friend who viewed her with the utmost kindness and affection. All the spectators were affected by the scene,

> an account of which soon spread thro' Paris, & by which I have no doubt, had a happy effect in promoting her discharge, which followed soon after.[6]

Madame de Lafayette was scheduled to face execution, but Elizabeth Monroe's deliberate act of bravery saved her from the blade, a demonstration of mercy hard to match.

An Open House: First Ladies and White House Visitors

If America had a dollar for every person who walked through the White House and shook hands with the First Lady, it could make the national debt disappear. It is reported that Pat Nixon personally greeted 250,000 people during her husband's first term alone. Many First Ladies have been criticized for maintaining a policy of equality in social events, but for people who never expected to meet a First Lady in her own home, it is an unforgettable moment and certainly an act of deliberate grace on her part.

Elizabeth Monroe

Elizabeth Monroe insisted on democratic informality in her entertaining, and some of her visitors were clearly surprised by the appearance of some others. In a report that probably is as much a tribute to the graciousness and thoughtfulness of Elizabeth Monroe as it is to the crass cleverness of the writer, one newspaper published this account regarding the Monroes' receptions:

> The secretaries, senators, foreign ministers, consuls, auditors, accountants, officers of the navy and army of every grade, farmers, merchants, parsons, priests, lawyers, judges, auctioneers, and nothin-

> garians—all with their wives and gawky offspring—crowd to the President's house every Wednesday evening; some in shoes, most in boots, and many in spurs; some snuffing, others chewing, and many longing for their cigars and whisky punch left at home; some with powdered heads, some frizzled and oiled; some whose head a comb has never touched, half hid by dirty collars, reaching far above their ears, as stiff as a pasteboard.[7]

Frances Cleveland

Frances Cleveland, at twenty-two the youngest of all our First Ladies, began holding informal receptions on Saturday afternoons for women in Washington. According to White House servant William Henry Crook, one adviser, who was concerned about the dignity of the role of First Lady, urged her to give them up because "about half of all the women who come Saturday afternoon are clerks from the department stores and others—a great rabble of shop-girls."

"Indeed!" said Mrs. Cleveland. "And if I should hold the little receptions some afternoon other than Saturday they couldn't attend, because they have to work all the other afternoons. Is that it?"

"Certainly. That's it exactly," the adviser said.

The President's wife responded by issuing orders to White House staff that nothing should ever again interfere with her Saturday afternoon receptions.[8]

Lucy Hayes

During the Hayes administration, according to Crook, British Minister Sir Edward Thornton and his entourage entered the White House and were shocked to discover Lucy sitting on the floor in front of an elderly veteran, who was seated on a sofa. The soldier, a veteran of the War of 1812, expected to have his picture taken in his dress uniform which he sent to the

White House ahead of him. However, the sergeant's stripes had not been attached, a fact that nearly brought the man to tears. Especially warmhearted to children and veterans, Lucy whipped out her sewing kit and made the repair herself—and it became a story that the veteran, the British minister, and Crook himself loved to tell.

Lucy also took a personal responsibility for the poor which, at first, stunned the White House staff. According to Thomas Pendel, the White House doorkeeper, notes came to the mansion from the destitute and poor wanting help. Lucy would ask him to come upstairs to see her, saying, "Mr. Pendel, here is some money, and here is a note. Take this and find out where they live, and give it to them."

William T. Crump, a White House steward, said he often took wagonloads of provisions to the poor in Washington. Whenever Lucy heard of an ill or destitute soldier, she was especially swift to investigate. In the case of a Major Bailey, whom they found suffering from disease and poverty, she sent a load of supplies and ordered Crump to buy furniture and bedclothes for his two rooms. At a cabinet meeting the next day she collected $125 for the benefit of the major and his family. According to Crump, Lucy and Rutherford's charitable contributions for January 1880 alone totaled $990, a remarkable sum for that time.

Abigail Fillmore

While she served as First Lady (from July 1851 to March 1853), Abigail Fillmore took up the cause of a blind and forgotten novelist, Mrs. S. Helen De Kroyft of New Orleans. A great lover of books and their writers, Abigail used her experiences as a former schoolteacher to create the first library in the White House.

Mrs. De Kroyft had been blind for seven long years before she began seeking help from Northern physicians. Someone took her to the White House for a visit with the First Lady, and Abigail became personally involved in the writer's cause, eventually introducing her to a Dr. Turnbull, who recently arrived in American from London.

In December 1852 the *New Orleans Daily Delta* printed Mrs. De Kroyft's open letter to the First Lady:

Dear Mrs. Fillmore,

I shall see again. Oh, I shall see again . . . for seven years a prisoner to darkness . . . and oh, how shall I ever find words to thank you for writing me to go to him. . . . Never, never shall I look on the flowers, or the white snow of winter, or the blue sky, but I shall remember to whom I owe it all. . . . You have made my heart glad, and now at last, you have turned my dark steps toward the light. . . . I thank you, I bless you, I love you, and all the time I shall pray for you.

Your most humble, most devoted friend,
S. Helen De Kroyft[9]

Support from the Sisters: First Ladies Helping Each Other

In her book *My Turn,* Nancy Reagan criticized Rosalynn Carter for not giving her a nice enough tour of the family quarters the first time she visited the White House after the 1980 election. Abigail Adams moaned because her daughter-in-law Louisa was not of Boston blood—and all of Washington criticized Elizabeth Monroe because she was no Dolley Madison.

Persecution is expected from the small-minded, from political opponents, and certainly from the media. But when it comes from within the ranks of the First Ladies themselves, it is a breach in the sorority. In fact, probably because of the painful bloodletting that occurs in the presidential campaigns, First Ladies often go out of the way to be gracious to one another, even when they are politically opposed.

Barbara Bush

After her husband lost to Bill Clinton in the 1992 election, Barbara Bush invited Hillary Clinton to the White House for a special tour of the family's private quarters. This is a standard gesture; however, Barbara welcomed

Hillary in a very public expression—with a warm embrace in front of reporters staked out on the South Lawn. "Avoid this crowd like the plague," she said, pointing to the press corps. "And if they quote you, make damn sure they heard you."

Lucy Hayes

At a White House reception in February 1878 Lucy Hayes asked Julia Tyler to assist her in receiving guests for the evening. Two more opposite First Ladies are hard to imagine, and this was a gesture of grace and reconciliation. Julia Gardiner Tyler was First Lady for only eight months after she married the widowed president—John Tyler, thirty years her senior—in 1844. She was just twenty-four, and historians often describe her as one who seemed a little too attached to colorful, almost regal socializing in the mansion.

The Tylers left the White House in 1845, and nearly fifteen years later, when President Tyler's native Virginia joined the Confederacy, he took an action that no president had taken before or since: With his wife's proud support, America's former president renounced and rebuked his allegiance to the United States and threw his efforts toward the rebel cause. Of their seven children (the last one born when he was in his seventies), the Tylers' two oldest sons served in the Confederate Army.

Lucy Hayes, who often seemed more articulate about the Union Army's mission than even Mary Lincoln or Julia Grant, certainly found the Tylers' action reprehensible. However, she greeted the widow Tyler with warmth and stood graciously next to her until all the guests were welcomed—a gesture surely not lost on anyone who walked through that receiving line.

Dolley Madison

Shortly after her husband became president in March 1845, Sarah Polk made a special trip to visit Dolley Madison, who was then about eighty. Joined by several other women who also came to see the affable former First

Lady known for her turbans, her memory for names, and her remarkable skill as White House hostess, Sarah Polk stood in exact contrast to the matriarch before her.

Dolley was naturally sociable and outgoing. Sarah was naturally serious and quiet.

Dolley served her husband best with her reputation for charming even his greatest political foes. Sarah served her husband as his personal secretary, typically matching his twelve-hour workdays.

Dolley was never more perfectly, thoroughly contented than when a White House party was in full swing. After a party in the spring of 1795, President Washington even said Dolley was the "sprightliest" dancing partner he had ever had.

By contrast, all dancing stopped at the inaugural ball when Mrs. Polk entered the room because guests knew her Moravian upbringing taught her it was sinful.

Regarding the spiritual themes of their lives, Dolley represented hospitality and acceptance of others; Sarah stood for accountability and stewardship. They were, however, exactly alike in their absolute devotion to their husbands.

So now, after moments of light chat between these two women of history, another visitor turned to Mrs. Polk and asked whether she would be paying calls on the ladies of Washington like Mrs. Madison did or whether—God forbid—she would become exclusive and only *receive* calls like that dreadful Mrs. Monroe.

Sarah deferred to Dolley for her opinion, and James Madison's widow made an observation that every First Lady has discovered on her own: She explained simply that customs—like politics—change. One can learn from the examples of others, she said, but—ultimately—she must find her own way through this experience. Mrs. Polk would have to decide for herself, Dolley concluded. With this, Sarah received from the grande dame of First Ladies—in front of women who would surely report the event—encouragement to put forth her own style, to trust her abilities, to be herself.

With this Dolley Madison laid a blessing on the head of Sarah Polk, who went back to the White House and did exactly what Dolley suggested.

Pat Nixon

In early 1971 the official Kennedy portraits were ready to be hung in the White House, and First Lady Pat Nixon—wanting to make certain the event was properly honored—wrote a private note to Jackie Kennedy Onassis to ask her wishes regarding a ceremony.

Jackie, who could not bring herself to return to the White House since she moved out after her husband's death, wrote to Pat, saying she simply did not have the courage to go through an official ceremony. She also did not want to bring her children back to the White House, she explained, because she dreaded the thought of exposing them publicly to the event.

Instead, Jackie suggested a private viewing, and Pat responded by arranging the plans and telling only four members of the White House staff—all sworn to strict secrecy. During their visit, Jackie and her children viewed the portraits before Tricia and Julie Nixon took John and Caroline Kennedy on a tour of the entire house.

After dinner President Nixon took John Kennedy into the Oval Office and showed him where he once played under his father's desk. Then Nixon took all the children to the Lincoln Bedroom and told them the legend that if you sit on the bed and make a wish, your wish will come true. In her letter to Patricia Nixon, Jackie Kennedy wrote that the day she dreaded turned out to be one of the most precious ones she ever spent with her children.

Elizabeth Monroe

Whenever Rachel Jackson traveled with her husband on national affairs, she seemed to fit in badly with his colleagues, especially during social events. A religious zealot who seemed genuinely uptight in most crowds (unless at Hermitage, their homestead in Nashville), Rachel was frumpy at best, demonstrated little interest in the state of government, and, as everyone knew, carried some dark secret regarding her first marriage. Rachel looked like a woman who had spent too much time on the frontier, showed little interest in fashion, and made a poor dancing partner, except in the adoring and passionate eyes of her husband. She simply did not fit in.

However, in 1824 President Monroe's genteel, well-bred, Virginia-born wife, who—in the shadow of Dolley Madison—became an outcast by Washington's social standards herself, saw something in the frontier woman that greatly appealed to her. Perhaps it was kinship in social rejection, but during an event in Washington the beautiful Elizabeth Monroe befriended the portly, lonely wife of Andrew Jackson, and the two corresponded warmly through their husbands until Rachel's death four years later.

Lady Bird Johnson

"This was a once-and-only day in the White House for us as hosts to the family who will succeed us here." So began Lady Bird Johnson's journal entry for Monday, November 11, 1968, in describing the four-hour visit she and her husband, Lyndon, had with Richard and Pat Nixon. "(Somehow, I could never call him Dick, but it is easy to call her Pat, because she was presiding officer of the Senate Ladies during eight years of my time there)," Lady Bird confessed. The visit included a cordial, lengthy exchange between the two men covering bureau appointments, Johnson's achievements for African Americans, the press, and the process of selecting Cabinet members.

Lady Bird took Pat on an extensive tour of the White House, gave as much helpful information as she could about the living quarters and the workings of her own office. She also spent a good deal of time trying to reassure Pat about the efficiency, devotion, and impersonal professionalism of the staff. "I think they have liked us, but we come and go, we presidents and First Ladies. That is as it should be. The first devotion of the staff must be to the White House and its workings.

"When we said good-bye at the diplomatic entrance, Pat kissed me. I was touched. Then they were gone. And so that was a major encounter—gracefully completed, I thought."[10]

There is an often-used sermon illustration I enjoy about a little boy running to the beach at dawn to rescue starfish. He knows the little creatures will die in the sun, and so he makes it his job to throw them back in the ocean. An old cynic sitting on the beach one day harps at the boy, "I don't know why you are doing that. It's a waste of time. You can't save them all, you know. What you are doing doesn't really make a difference."

"It's true, I can't save them all," says the boy, holding up one and admiring it, "but I can save this one, and it sure makes a difference to him."

We aren't always certain our actions make a difference, but this little boy—and the collective, courageous, inspiring acts of our First Ladies—speak boldly to us: In the eyes of God, an act of mercy is never a wasted gesture.

Echoes of This Beatitude in the Bible

Isaiah 40:1: "Comfort, comfort my people says your God."

I Kings 8:23: "O Lord, God of Israel, there is no God like you in heaven above or on earth below—you who keep your covenant of love with your servants who continue wholeheartedly in your way."

Psalm 6:2: "Be merciful to me, Lord, for I am faint; O Lord, heal me, for my bones are in agony."

Psalm 23:6: "Surely goodness and love will follow me all the days of my life, and I will dwell in the house of the Lord forever."

Psalm 31:7: "I will be glad and rejoice in your love, for you saw my affliction and knew the anguish of my soul."

Psalm 86:13: "For great is your love toward me: you have delivered my soul from the depths of the grave."

Matthew 23:23: "Woe to you, teachers of the law and Pharisees, you hypocrites! You give a tenth of your spices—mint, dill and cummin. But you have neglected the more important matters of the law—justice, mercy and faithfulness. You should have practiced the latter, without neglecting the former."

Matthew 12:7: "If you had known what these words mean, 'I desire mercy, not sacrifice,' you would not have condemned the innocent."

Psalm 123:3: "Have mercy on us, O Lord, have mercy on us, for we have endured much contempt."

First Lady Quotables

"Even when people can't speak your language, they can tell if you have love in your heart."

—A quote by Pat Nixon when she was First Lady; this appears on her tombstone as well

"For several years, you've had impressed upon you the importance to your career of dedication and hard work. This is true, but as important as your obligations as a doctor, lawyer or business leader will be, you are a human being first, and those human connections—with spouses, with children, with friends—are the most important investments you will ever make."

—Barbara Bush to students at Wellesley College

"A traveller between life and death
The reason firm. The temperate will
Endurance, foresight, strength and skill
A perfect woman nobly planned
To warn, to comfort and command
And yet a spirit still and bright
With something of angelic light"

—The tombstone of Ellen Axson Wilson

Photo on page 126:

Pat Nixon loved children, especially the disadvantaged and underprivileged. Here she celebrates Christmas at the White House holding a little girl.

Photo courtesy of Nixon Presidential Materials, National Archives

Blessed are the pure in heart, for they will see God.

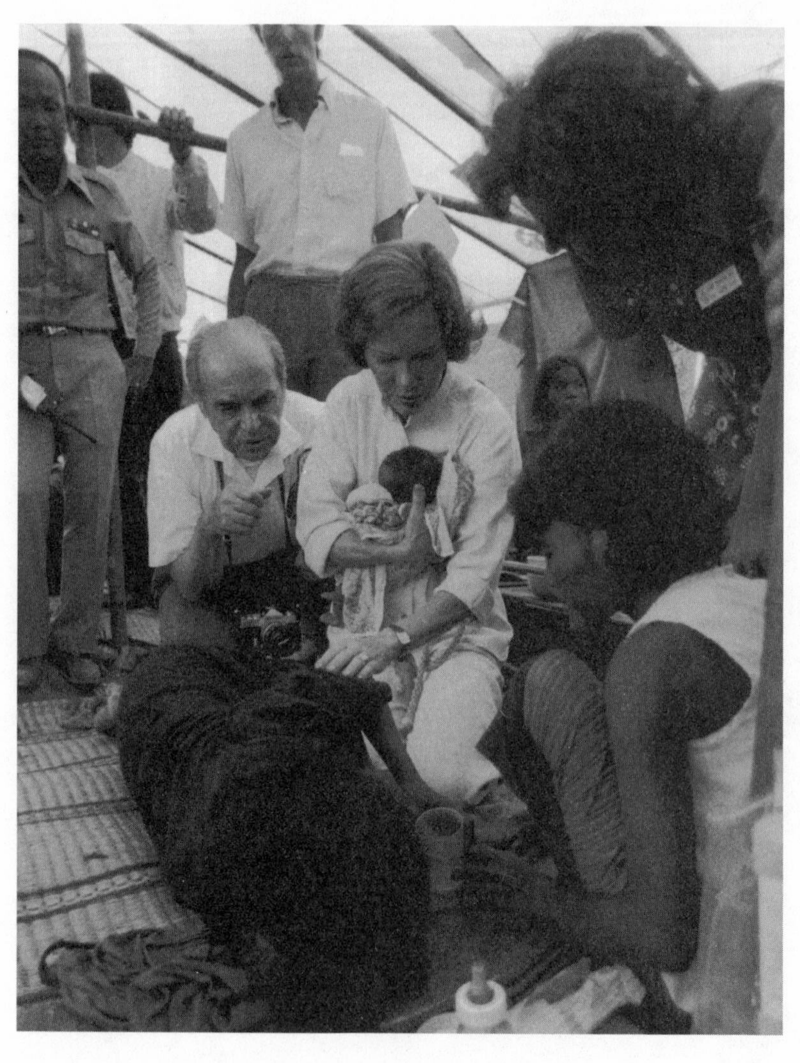

Rosalynn Carter

Chapter Six

Blessed are the pure in heart,

for they will see God.

First Ladies of Pure Heart

Announce in your sanctuary or Sunday school classroom that today's lesson is based strictly on the sixth Beatitude, and you will lose half your audience. This one sentence from the Bible can distance or intimidate readers as effectively as the mind-numbing list of Christ's ancestors at the start of Matthew's Gospel or the metaphoric and badly abused book of Revelation.

The problem with the phrase "pure in heart" is the superhuman standard—the near-perfect performance—it seems to imply through today's translation. Women especially interpret this as meaning "always kind, giving, and warm-hearted while serving God." This is an absolute impossibility in almost any spiritual journey. Adult scriptural students typically offer two quick responses to the phrase: They dismiss it entirely for its absurdity or they respond with those emotionally deadly "shoulds" and "oughts." One friend said, "I should work harder on this point. I really ought to be kinder and more dedicated." This from a woman whose service to her church, her family, and the local homeless shelter already left her with little time for herself.

Pure in heart is not perfect grace, perfect composure, or perfect faith. Pure of heart does not mean making the journey with an unweathered countenance and unruffled skirts (Now *there's* an albatross). It means making the journey in the first place, and it is best translated as "single-mindedness" with your sights always pointed toward God.

Jacob's mystical nocturnal encounter with God in the book of Genesis serves as a helpful image for anyone wanting to understand this Beatitude: Wrestling until dawn, struggling with the agony of disjointed bones yet holding firmly to his aggressor, Jacob claimed victory when God cried, "Let go of me!" "First you must give me a blessing," Jacob screamed. Then God renamed Jacob, calling him Israel, and the God of all creation blessed him. This is the first time the name of Israel is mentioned in scripture. Jacob's wrestling with God was the moment of birth for a nation defined by covenant, heirship, and its perceptive writings on the universal nature of human spirituality.

Pairing Jacob's story with the sixth Beatitude brings some dramatic instruction: Wrestle with God. Wrestle with your faith. Wrestle with the religious lessons you learned from your parents and scripture. Set your sights on God, and demand from God the blessings of a dedicated servant. The greatest blessings—which came to Jacob and come today to those who are pure in heart—are spiritual illumination, wisdom, and the possibility of establishing a legacy in which our actions extend far beyond our own lives.

The meaning of "pure in heart" for the First Ladies is a mix of courage and controversy, definition and paradox. This is true for the larger population as people have practiced their religion throughout American history, and especially in light of our nation's First Ladies. Causes one person may choose to take on in the spirit of Christ's teachings may be directly opposed to those chosen by another. For instance, all Christians do not stand on the same side of political issues such as abortion, gay rights, immigration, the death penalty, and an individual's right to choose when to die. Therefore, being pure in heart hinges on single-minded obedience to God and not on being politically correct.

Three of the women selected for this chapter represent this Beatitude particularly well for their epoch in American history. In their own way, these women serve as images that help us understand the unique influence American women have had on the religious development of our country. Anna Harrison was the westward pioneer of the 1790s, Sarah Polk was the nineteenth-century settler representing temperance, industry, and piety, and Rosalynn Carter is today's traditional and moderate Christian who actually represents more American women than any outspoken fundamental conservative can accurately claim.

Rosalynn Carter

In the last several years I have written a great deal about Rosalynn Carter, and one impression always sticks with me: Rosalynn's religious journey is a delightful blueprint for women of traditional and moderate religious views who are trying to balance those elements with a dedication to full partnership within marriage and to community service. Any woman today who has to juggle work, family, church, and even one public service project would do well to learn from Rosalynn's example. In fact, Rosalynn is an icon for anyone trying to hold tightly to traditional values and the Bible in one hand and a gavel, committee roster, and day planner in the other.

In her autobiography, *First Lady from Plains,* Rosalynn describes her thorough religious training as a child and how God was a very real presence in her life. She was taught to love God, and she grew up determined to live the kind of life God would want. That meant, among other things, to love the people around her, to be kind, and to help those in need. She once told me, "I was taught growing up that everyone you ministered to was important, that every person and every act was significant. I listen to Jimmy every Sunday [in his Sunday school class at their church] talk about Jesus and the things He did on earth and how He taught us to walk in His footsteps and then comes the question, 'What does it mean to take care of those who are poor and suffering and sometimes even despised by others?' "

In American history she will be remembered for her contribution to the Mideast Peace Accords that her husband brokered between Egyptian president Anwar Sadat and Israeli prime minister Menachem Begin at Camp David in September 1979. She will also be noted for her international childhood immunization program and her dedication to the elderly. Rosalynn's advocacy of the mentally ill and mentally retarded won her a presidential citation from the American Psychological Association, prompted her appointment as an honorary fellow by the American Psychiatric Association, and the National Mental Health Association even named her Volunteer of the Decade. All these achievements were born of her religious convictions, namely, that she had both the obligation and skill to improve the lives of people around her, convictions developed in childhood.

Rosalynn grew up in Plains, Georgia, a very small town in a very rural county, and one whose social life centered on church and school. "My grandmother Murray was Lutheran, my grandfather Baptist, and my parents Methodist," she wrote in her autobiography. "I went to all three churches almost every time the doors opened, it seemed—to Sunday school and regular church services, to prayer meeting, Methodist League, Baptist Girls Auxiliary, and Bible School."[1] During her childhood the big event of the year—which still happens annually in Plains, Georgia—was the revival. For an entire week there was preaching morning and night. Rosalynn's family never missed a service, and the preachers always went to her parents' home for a meal.

In July 1946 Rosalynn Smith married her hometown sweetheart, Jimmy Carter, and began her tenure as a navy wife. In the next seven years she would become the mother of three boys and live in Virginia, Connecticut, Hawaii, and California before her father-in-law was diagnosed with cancer and Jimmy resigned his commission to return home to take over his father's business. When they returned to Plains, their social lives revolved around the Plains Baptist Church, where they were members, Sunday school teachers, and volunteers for most events. Carter won a seat in the Georgia state Senate before claiming the governor's mansion in 1970, where Rosalynn began her service to mental illness and mental retardation by reforming the state's system of service. She also took on broader health care issues, civil rights, and even tackled the odious, politically unpopular issue of prison reform.

"Problems that come to a president or a governor are the difficult ones. After all, if they are easier to solve, they're solved before they get to the governor's desk or the president's desk," she said. "One thing that greatly impresses you when you're in the governor's mansion or the White House is just how many problems there are and how many people suffer. The problems you see are the problems that never go away—like the problem of the poor, and the handicapped, and the refugees. These are problems that are just so enormous, and I think you just have to trust God to guide you. So you assume some responsibility, and you ask, 'Why am I in this position?' 'What is expected of me?' 'What can I do to help?'

"What you can do is the *best* you can do," Rosalynn says. "You seek guidance from God to do what's right and best. . . . I think if you are deeply rooted in your faith before you get there, it is a lot easier. I was always so thankful for growing up in the church. I don't see how anybody without faith could maintain any kind of stability or equilibrium when those things happen to you. I think if you do have a deep religious faith then you just fall back on it."

After about eighteen months in the Georgia governor's mansion, Rosalynn found herself overwhelmed and depressed. She decided to join a Bible class and, in that class, learned that a well-known evangelist was scheduled to teach a course on Christian living—a mistake from the moment she walked into the room. The pastor taught that wives should be absolutely, totally subservient to their husbands. He said children should be completely controlled by their fathers as well, and ignored the concept of mutual respect and sharing and love within the family. "Subservience and discipline," she wrote. "There's more to life than that, I thought, and there's more to living the life Jesus wants us to live than being punishing and rigid and afraid. . . . I got up and left."[2]

Feeling guilty and assuming she was perhaps the one who misunderstood, Rosalynn went back once more. This time she managed to stay for twenty minutes. Soon after this, though, a friend from that same Bible class asked Rosalynn if she could go to the mansion and speak to the trustees (inmates who served as servants and groundskeepers) about Jesus. "I was glad to have her come," Rosalynn wrote. "The prisoners might need Jesus, and I needed Him, too. I especially needed to be reassured after my conflict with the evangelist. Had she sensed that? I'll never know." As Rosalynn listened to her friend's speech about releasing one's problems to Jesus, which concluded, "He will help us if only we will let Him," Rosalynn's response was as firm as anyone else in the room. "That's what was wrong. I'd clung to all my problems and not let them go. . . . That was the key. Release! Release! And I had forgotten to do that. . . . It was a burden lifted. Things didn't change suddenly. It took a while for me to work through all the problems I'd saved for myself. . . . But that experience and that lesson saved my life. I have been in many situations since that were difficult, that could have been very lonely and defeating, but I am constantly aware that God is with me to help through the difficult times."[3]

When the Carters lost the presidential election of 1980, they returned to Plains and built a postpresidential life of public service absolutely unrivaled by other chief executives and First Ladies. "When we came home from the White House we realized we still had vast resources," she said. "I mean anybody will help you with anything because you were president. All you have to do is ask them, and that puts a huge responsibility on what you do with that power. Especially because of our Christian religion, I think it was important to us to help those less fortunate. It was the religious underpinnings which motivated us in this direction—to create the Carter Center—when we realized we had this kind of influence. Then it developed into something we never dreamed it would be."

The center is located about two miles from downtown Atlanta on a thirty-five-acre site, and it includes four circular, interconnected pavilions totaling nearly 100,000 square feet of space. The center has an annual budget of nearly $26 million, as well as 250 full-time employees and another hundred student interns. While the bulk of employees work in Atlanta, the center also has representatives in Guyana, Liberia, Ethiopia, and Nicaragua. Through her office there, Rosalynn oversees many of her own long-standing programs, including the Mental Health Task Force and the Every Child by Two program, designed to get every single child around the globe immunized by age two.

A former Sunday school teacher, she volunteers regularly at Maranatha Baptist Church, in Plains, where she and her husband have been members since leaving the White House in 1981. With her Bible in one hand and day planner in the other, Rosalynn represents millions of women throughout the United States today who are making a difference in their families, their churches, and their communities by dedicating themselves to the same themes that surface in her life. One of those themes has been articulated often by her husband in the adult Sunday school class he teaches there: "If we are going to define ourselves by Christian standards, we have an obligation to frequently examine our relationship with God. If we find anything interfering with that relationship, we are meant to address it immediately." Now, *that* is pure in spirit.

Hannah Van Buren

"She was a sincere Christian, a dutiful child, tender mother, affectionate wife. Precious shall be the memory of her virtues."

—Tombstone of Hannah Van Buren

Precious is the memory of her virtues, but precious few are the details of the thirty-six years of her life. Hannah Van Buren, gone eighteen years before her husband won the presidential election of 1836, is a hazy, incomplete footnote in American history, and the stories about her leave one pleading for more facts and fewer adjectives. The handful of details that *are* known about her life, however, make her the perfect example of Christ's sixth Beatitude as it gets interpreted in its narrowest form—the absence of spiritual defilement or pollution.

Born March 8, 1783, in New York, she came from eight generations of pure Holland ancestry, and she grew up in the Dutch Reformed Church, a kinder, gentler branch of Calvinism. She married Martin Van Buren February 21, 1807, in a ceremony performed in her sister's home. The bridegroom was twenty-five, an attorney who had even served as clerk for two years in New York City for a notable law firm. She was twenty-four. (During the twelve years they were married, they spoke Dutch within their own household.) Their first son was born at the very end of 1807.

The next year Martin's career moved them to Hudson. Seven years later, she joined the First Presbyterian Church, which was headed by Rev. John Chester. With no Dutch Reformed congregation in Hudson, this was the closest alternative. In their nine years there, Hannah gave birth to two hardy boys and a third child, who apparently died as an infant.

In 1817 the Van Burens moved to Albany, where the future president served as state's attorney. They joined the Second Presbyterian Church, apparently without hesitation, because their Rev. Chester from Hudson had been transferred to this church shortly before the Van Burens moved to the city.

When the pastor organized a Sunday school in Albany "to teach the unlettered waifs of the street to read," most women of the church opposed the plan. Since the founding of America, Protestant "Sunday school" almost always has meant an education program for one's own members, especially children, within one's own church. Chester was actually proposing a community outreach program closely aligned with the original intent of Sunday school as first developed in England in 1780, when newspaper editor Robert Raikes of Gloucester hired women to teach poor children—who worked six days a week and lived in hovels—how to read and write and improve their lives. What began as a secular program eventually changed into a vehicle of Christian education.

Women of Chester's church were not rejecting the education of their own children. They were rejecting a plan to help the city's poorest children. Hannah Van Buren, however, according to Rev. Chester, "warmly supported the project," a response that seems to have drawn his absolute devotion to her, and he is the likely author of the obituary of Hannah Van Buren, which appeared in the Albany *Argus*, February 8, 1819.

It is not likely she was able to do much herself to teach those needy children because these were the final months of her life, and she was confined by a pregnancy that would produce a fourth strapping Van Buren male in the hard, bitter winter of 1818 to 1819. She herself died just weeks later, on February 5, the official cause, tuberculosis.

Rev. Chester's obituary for Hannah Van Buren, with its flowery reflections and heaping sweet praise, is a perfect period piece. Yet, given the other handful of details we know of her life, it probably was easily and sincerely composed.

> Died in this city . . . Mrs. Hannah Van Buren . . . in the thirty-sixth year of her age. . . . As a daughter and a sister, wife and mother, her loss is deeply deplored, for in all these varied relations, she was affectionate, tender and truly estimable. But the tear of sorrow is almost dried by the reflection that she lived possessing the

> most engaging simplicity of manners, her heart was for the wants and sufferings of others. Her temper was uncommonly mild and sweet, her bosom was filled with benevolence and content—no love of show, no ambitious desires, no pride of ostentation ever disturbed its peace. . . . Humility was her crowning grace, she possessed it in rare degree; it took root and flourished full and fair, shedding over every act of her life its genial influence. She was an ornament of the Christian faith. . . .[4]

Martin Van Buren, the eighth president, outlived his wife by forty-two years. Just a short while before his death, which occurred in 1862, he wrote an 800-page autobiography but never once mentioned Hannah, wanting to leave a purely political but not personal account of his role in American history. (His sons are referred to only if they participated in some public affair.) So, instead, historians are left to draw conclusions about his devotion to Hannah from the fact that Van Buren never remarried.

In regard to its spiritual and religious implications, the story of Hannah Van Buren poses many frustrations because it represents an almost impossible level of performance and leaves the reader wanting to say, "Even Christ got angry. Moses smashed the Ten Commandments in a fit of rage."

Didn't Hannah get miffed when the other women of her church refused to help the pastor? Wasn't she furious when she realized she herself would not live to raise those boys? Wasn't she even tempted to curse at God while spitting up blood in a consumptive's fit? Did she ever have one thing to repent for? Not that we can see from history.

Hannah Van Buren represents the sixth Beatitude when it is understood as "the absence of spiritual defilement." I only wish we knew more about her.

Sarah Polk

Virginia-born First Ladies—who already had the land, the name, the heritage—also had an Episcopal church that saw them through birth, death, personal sacrifice, and constant service. But Sarah Childress was influenced by the Moravians and their religious cousins, the Presbyterians, and that meant greater emphasis on industry, specific direction on just how to shape one's religious and financial environment, and strict abstinence regarding drink, dance, and cards. While this could be an oppressive mantle for even the most well-intentioned student of Christ's teachings, Sarah wore it with ease.

John Quincy Adams once described John Polk as a man who "had no wit, no literature, no point of argument, no gracefulness of delivery, no elegance of language, no philosophy, no pathos, no felicitous impromptus, nothing that can qualify an orator."[5] However, Sarah found a spiritual mate, a man of great business and political possibilities and a genuine *partner.* Regarding his time in the White House, Polk confided to an associate that no one knew his presidential affairs better than his own wife. Unlike Rachel Jackson, Anna Harrison, and Margaret Taylor, Sarah Polk *wanted* to be in the White House. By all accounts, she was the first genuine politically minded First Lady since Abigail Adams. But unlike Abigail, Sarah worked literally at her husband's side from morning to night.

Like Elizabeth Monroe and Frances Cleveland, Sarah opened the White House weekly with informal receptions for common citizens and not just for the elite. In social events that did include the decision makers, she was conversational and observant but careful not to reveal her own political views. In commenting on the affairs of state—which she understood as clearly as her husband did, incidentally—she would begin, "Mr. Polk feels . . ." Inside the White House, however, without timidity or hesitation, she made her presence known by swiftly ditching three social customs—serving alcohol, dancing at receptions, and receiving visitors on Sunday. In the early months of Polk's term, more than one administration official had the bad timing—or good, depending on his religious interests—of showing up to discuss one quick issue with the president on the Sabbath, only to have Mrs. Polk pointedly invite him to join them for church at First Presbyterian.

The joke in Washington was that one Sunday morning she said to a visitor, "I understand there is a fine new preacher at the pulpit," and he responded, "Then I would like to go with you, for I have played cards with him many a time!" But if Washington was rolling its eyes at her predilections by nicknaming her "Sahara Sarah," the rapidly developing American heartland was cheering her religious nature, because she represented many of the nation's citizens in ways that Washington society did not.

As American Protestantism swept westward, it carried the same agenda of industry, thrift, temperance, and piety that Sarah and John Polk held. The Nashville *Union* hailed "her dignified and exemplary deportment since her occupancy of the Presidential Mansion. . . . As a professor of religion [that is, one who professes to be religious], doubtless Mrs. Polk deeply realized the responsibility of her position. . . . The example of Mrs. Polk can hardly fail of exerting . . . a salutary influence. . . . All will agree that by the exclusion of frivolities and her excellent deportment in other respects, she has conferred additional dignity upon the executive department of our government."[6]

But human spirituality is nothing if not ironic. Sarah Polk not only believed in predestination and the spiritual disciplines of ritual, prayer, and personal piety, she also believed in slavery. The Polks brought two slaves with them into the White House and had up to forty on their plantation in Yalobusha County, Mississippi. Though apparently humane in the treatment of their "servants," John and Sarah Polk participated in that standard Southern economic system of increasing profits on the backs of slaves, apparently without much of a twinge in conscience. While north of the Mason-Dixon line, American Protestantism interpreted slavery under very *different* views, in the Southern Methodist, Presbyterian, and Episcopal churches it was for the most part accepted as a deeply entrenched element to the economic stability of a plantation or business. John and Sarah were clearly products of a Southern upbringing.

John Polk was born in 1795 in North Carolina, graduated from the University of North Carolina in 1818, and moved to Tennessee, where he practiced law. He married Sarah in 1824, and entered the United States House of Representatives the following year, taking his new bride into Washington. Because the couple had no children, Sarah could involve herself more fully in her husband's career, and both were such devoted Democrats, she referred to President Jackson as "Uncle Andrew." A tireless worker during seven consecutive terms in Congress, John Polk missed only one day of work. Eventually he became governor of Tennessee.

During the Democratic Convention of 1844, Martin Van Buren failed to carry enough delegates, and John Polk became the first dark horse to enter a race for the White House. In the general election he faced Henry Clay, who was later remembered for his famous quote that year, "I'd rather be right than President." He got his wish, and John Polk entered the White House with Sarah as his right hand.

Politically, she wholly endorsed her husband's expansionist policy, which led to the war with Mexico in 1846 and the eventual acquisition of parts of present-day Arizona, California, Colorado, Nevada, Utah, and Wyoming. While his supporters saluted this achievement, his opponents—including an Illinois congressman named Lincoln—challenged the act as pure aggression. During his one term (he made it clear he would serve only one term), he acquired large amounts of territory, reduced market tariffs, and established a new independent treasury—all with Sarah's constant support and advice.

Meanwhile the Polks' piety made its presence known so effectively, it became the subject of international news on more than one occasion. When an Austrian dignitary called at the White House on a Sunday to present credentials, servants were told to inform him the president "declined seeing company on the Sabbath but would be pleased to see him tomorrow." The story also is told that one night at a White House reception a bold South Carolina man approached Mrs. Polk and said, "Madame, I have long wished to see the lady upon whom the Bible pronounces a woe!" Mrs. Polk looked puzzled and several people gasped. Then the man explained, "Does not the Bible say, 'Woe unto you when all men shall speak well of you?' " A corny joke at best, but the element of truth is present: Sarah Polk was a pious woman whose religious nature struck a chord with many Americans.

Martha Washington

Upon Martha Washington's death, one newspaper wrote: "To those amiable and Christian virtues which adorn the female character, she added the dignity of manners, superiority of understanding, a mind intelligent and elevated. The silence of respectful grief is our best eulogy."[7] This tribute in May 1802 says as much about the historic and religious role of women in our early history as it does about our first president's wife. Like Rev.

Chester's obituary of Hannah Van Buren, this is a classic remembrance. Surely it was written by someone who hoped "this great democratic experiment" known as the United States would last for centuries and that Martha would be the first of many presidential wives. However, it must be noted that despite the historian's tendency to set aside her religious faith, Martha Washington was indeed a woman who earnestly sought to reflect to all around her what she felt God wanted her to be. Family worship was a part of her regular routine, and in her later years Martha often retired early so her granddaughter could read scripture to her before bedtime.

Betty Ford

On June 22, 1976, First Lady Betty Ford was attending a dinner hosted by the Jewish National Fund of America at the Hilton Hotel in New York, when Dr. Maurice Sage, president of the organization, had a heart attack and collapsed. In the confusion, while Secret Service agents worked on the dying man, Betty Ford took the microphone and calmly asked, "Can we all bow our heads for a moment for Rabbi Sage? He is going to the hospital and needs our prayers. Would you rise and bow your heads."

She said in prayer, "Dear Father in Heaven, we know you can take care of him, we know you can bring him back to us. You are our leader. You are our strength. You are what life is all about. Love and love of fellow man is what we all need and depend on. . . ." Then she asked everyone in the room—which totaled about three thousand—to pray privately. Sage died shortly after reaching the hospital. Betty later wrote: "I've been highly praised for the way I behaved on that night at the Hilton, but I don't think praise is warranted. What I did was instinctive, not an act of will."[8]

Anna Harrison

Anna Symmes Harrison is distinguished in American annals because her husband was the first president to die in office, and she herself held the shortest tenure of any First Lady. In many ways she is described with the same phrases that apply to other presidents' wives—"trained well in social graces, born to a family of good standing, a woman of physical beauty." But in the field of American women's studies, Anna Harrison is an absolute standout in one regard: She is an icon for the thousands of women who traveled westward during the early life of our nation—women willing to test their own hardiness, faith, and tenacity in the cruel and crude unsettled world far beyond civilization, women who took their religion westward and created the first log-hewed churches in America's heartland.

Born into a family that provided security, wealth, and position, Anna Symmes was four years old when her mother died in 1779. Soon thereafter her father, Judge John Cleves Symmes, left her in the care of her grandparents on the eastern tip of Long Island while he traveled west to oversee an extremely successful venture in land development.

In her early years Anna enjoyed an especially thorough education. In fact, after William Henry Harrison's death in 1841, it would be another thirty-five years—with Lucy Hayes's arrival in Washington—before America would have another First Lady as thoroughly educated in religion and the liberal arts as Anna Harrison. She attended the Clinton Academy as a girl before entering a highly respected boarding school in New York City. Schoolmistress Isabella Graham, who oversaw Anna's education there, arrived in New York in 1789 at the personal invitation of the Reverend Dr. John Witherspoon.[9] He was the minister who signed the Declaration of Independence, served as president of what would become Princeton University, and carried John Calvin's theology with such vigor, he almost single-handedly organized Presbyterianism in America. It is safe to say Anna Harrison's religious training was nothing if not thorough.

By the time she arrived at the banks of the Ohio on January 1, 1795, to begin her new life with her father and stepmother, nineteen-year-old Anna Symmes was a young woman of beauty and grace. Shortly after her arrival she met William Henry Harrison, a man whose future political opponents would associate with hard cider and log cabins, but a man who actually grew up amid wealth and culture as she had. He was the son of Benjamin Harrison, an intimate friend of George Washington's, a signer of the Declaration of Independence, a member of the First Continental Congress, and a man who once served as governor of the state.

By birth he was an aristocrat, by occupation a soldier, and by presidential appointment William Henry Harrison was the indefatigable guardian and godhead of that vast backwoods known as the great Northwest Territory. He ruled for twelve years the remarkable domain that would eventually become Ohio, Indiana, Michigan, Illinois, and Wisconsin. Before there were streams of westward pioneers, before there was any real semblance of civilization in that "land beyond the mountains," even before there were Methodist itinerants, Anna Harrison entered the magnificent, devastating adventure that belonged to the earliest explorers when she got married on November 25, 1795.

A westward pioneer became larger than life in the eyes of provincial New England and genteel Virginia. He was broader, more daring and vigorous than easterners. "They were the children of the Revolution and they sought to put into their lives and the social structures they created the ideals for which the Revolution stood," wrote historian James A. Green. "In this they differed greatly from the East where naturally society was more fixed and less easily changed."[10]

While her husband carried out his duties as secretary of the Northwest Territory, territorial governor of Indiana, and major general in the War of 1812, Anna Harrison lived often in isolation with their growing family (they had ten children) in Vincennes, Indiana. She fought bears and Indians, created a school for her children, and saw to their religious instruction as well. By 1815 the family moved back to the Harrison homestead in North Bend, and in 1819 the Harrisons were among a group who started the Presbyterian church at Cleves, located one mile from North Bend. They contributed boards from their own sawmill to help build it, assisted the pastor with housing, and regularly held luncheons at their home after the Sunday services.

According to one biographer, the future president was typically on hand to greet a new pastor to the church and wasn't afraid to offer suggestions about the congregation. In the case of Rev. Horace Bushnell, "The general told him that in the cities it was all very well for a minister to use long words, and to quote Latin and Greek, but when he was in the country he advised him in his preaching to 'shoot low and aim straight.' " On another occasion the general was working with a gardener pruning grapevines, when the hired hand suggested the general get a watchdog to keep the bad boys in the area away from the grapes. "The general said he did not think much of a watch dog, but believed a Sunday school teacher would be a better remedy 'as in that case both the grapes and the boys would be saved.' "[11]

This story speaks as much of Anna as her husband, for they were cut from the same religious bolt of cloth. In a letter to her cousin, Mrs. Phoebe R. Reeve, dated November 12, 1834, Anna wrote: "The state of religion is quite low in this place. I cannot but think that President Jackson's Administration has been a very great curse to America by taking off people's minds from religious subjects, particularly men—but perhaps I am doing wrong to make this observation as your good husband may be a supporter of the President. If so, I ask his pardon as everyone has a right to judge for themselves." She ended the letter, "May the Almighty bless you."[12]

Catherina Van Rensselaer, daughter of General Solomon Van Rensselaer of New York, accompanied her father on a westward journey in July 1840 that included a visit to the Harrison homestead in North Bend. She described the location as "a beautiful spot, and 'the cabin' stands back some distance. . . . This is a spacious and convenient dwelling. Mrs. Harrison is one of the handsomest old ladies I have ever seen—she is perfect in beauty and such a good person I love her dearly."[13]

Less is known about Anna Harrison than most other First Ladies, yet more is known about her than the thousands of pioneering women she represents. It is a certainty, however, that Anna felt more akin to those God-fearing westward adventurers than she ever did the ladies of Washington.

The sixth Beatitude represents a private, intimate, life-changing journey back to the purity of God. Imagine that you are running a race with all your ancestors, friends and family lining the streets to cheer your efforts and encourage you across the finish line. Imagine the anguish of absolute isolation, physical pain, and disorientation. As understood by this Beatitude, the journey back to God is both of these extremes. The promise of spiritual illumination, according to Christ and demonstrated in the lives of our First Ladies, makes much of the journey an adventure that produces spiritual strength and wisdom. As we focus our sights on God, let us hold on to the examples of these women who so clearly represent the heart and soul of the nation.

Echoes of This Beatitude in the Bible

Psalm 51:10: "Create in me a pure heart, O God, and renew a steadfast spirit within me."

Acts 15:8–9: "God, who knows the heart, showed that he accepted them by giving the Holy Spirit to them, just as he did to us. He made no distinction between us and them, for he purified their hearts by faith."

Job 16:17: "Yet my hands have been free of violence and my prayer is pure."

Zephaniah 3:9: "Then I will purify the lips of the peoples, that all of them may call on the name of the Lord and serve him shoulder to shoulder."

Philippians 4:8 "Finally, brothers, whatever is true, whatever is noble, whatever is right, whatever is pure, whatever is lovely, whatever is admirable—if anything is excellent or praiseworthy—think about such things."

I Timothy 1:5: "The goal of this command is love, which comes from a pure heart and a good conscience and a sincere faith."

Hebrews 10:22: "Let us draw near to God with a sincere heart in full assurance of faith, having our hearts sprinkled to cleanse us from a guilty conscience and having our bodies washed with pure water."

James 1:27: "Religion that God our Father accepts as pure and faultless is this: to look after orphans and widows in their distress and to keep oneself from being polluted by the world."

James 3:17: "But the wisdom that comes from heaven is first of all pure; then peace-loving, considerate, submissive, full of mercy and good fruit, impartial and sincere."

First Lady Quotables

"George Bush and I have been the two luckiest people in the world, and when all the dust is settled and all the crowds are gone, the things that matter are faith, family and friends. We have been inordinately blessed, and we know that."

—Barbara Bush

Watch-Fires

Love was not given the human heart
For careless dealing.
Its spark was lit that man
Might know Divine revealing.

Heaped up with sacrificial brands
The flame, in mounting,
Enkindles other hearts with love
Beyond the counting.

Reflected back into each life,
These vast fires, glowing
Do then become the perfect love
Of Christ's bestowing.

—Grace Coolidge

Photo on page 152:

Touched by the pain and suffering of Southeast Asia, Rosalynn Carter (center) cradles a dying infant and comforts the girl's mother during her visit to a Cambodian refugee camp in Thailand, November 1979.

Photo courtesy of the Jimmy Carter Library

Blessed are the peacemakers, for they will be called sons of God.

Eleanor Roosevelt

CHAPTER SEVEN

Blessed are the peacemakers,

for they will be called sons of God.

First Ladies as Peacemakers

"What can one woman do to prevent war? This is the question that comes my way in any number of letters these days."

So began Eleanor Roosevelt's column *My Day* on December 20, 1961.

If the woman in question is one of our First Ladies, she's considered this point a great deal. Jimmy Carter insists his wife, Rosalynn, has been his full partner in all their peace efforts from the Camp David Accords in 1978 to negotiations in Haiti, North Korea, and Bosnia in 1994. Julia Grant offered to cross enemy lines under a flag of truce to try to win an end to the Civil War. Edith Roosevelt secretly contributed to the successful peace accord her husband, Theodore, negotiated between Russia and Japan in 1905—an accord that earned him the Nobel Peace Prize.

Eleanor herself responded to the question with a righteous obsession regarding the spiritual elements of equality, justice, and human dignity. Franklin Roosevelt's wife was not necessarily a beautiful woman, but she carried herself with the poise, dignity, and ease of one who knew she was dedicated to the right causes—and there was no cause more precious to Eleanor than human rights. In this regard, peace is not defined as the absence of tension. It is the search for justice, equality, and basic human rights such as the freedom of speech, the right to work, to decent housing and education, and the right to adequate food supplies and medical care. On another level, a peacemaker is one who tries to either end or prevent conflict through negotiations and a position of strength. If the First Ladies had a single voice on this issue, it would say, "I have seen war's ravages, and I am a pacifist, but I also know there are times when war is inevitable."

Eleanor Roosevelt

Eleanor's greatest gift to the world was the Universal Declaration of Human Rights, an international document created within the United Nations. The first intergovernmental bill of rights and fundamental freedoms, the document was created to identify and protect the dignity and rights of each human on the planet. The name "United Nations" was used during World War II to identify the countries allied against Germany, Italy, and Japan. At the end of 1945 it was adopted as the name of the postwar world alliance whose primary purpose has been maintaining international peace and security. As leader of one of the Big Four powers (the United States, the United Kingdom, China, and the Soviet Union), Franklin Roosevelt was heavily involved in the organization's creation and development from 1942 until his death in April 1945.

In early December 1945, President Truman asked Eleanor to serve as a United States delegate for the first meeting of the United Nations Assembly in London. In her column on December 21, 1945, she explained that the request came to her "largely because my husband laid the foundations for the organization through which we all hope to build world peace. . . . Some things I can take to the first meeting: A sincere desire to understand the problems of the rest of the world and our relationship to them; a real goodwill for people throughout the world; a hope that I shall be able to build a sense of personal trust and friendship with my co-workers, for without that understanding our work would be doubly difficult."

Eleanor also took along her achievements and position as former First Lady, a remarkable, tireless capacity for work and a modesty not shared by all her coworkers. "He is able," she wrote about one of her colleagues, "but so many foibles! All these important men have them, however. I'm so glad I never feel important, it does complicate life!"[1]

While serving as a delegate she dealt with some who wanted to transform the United Nations into a world government, and she joined with the relatively small number of women delegates to issue a discreet manifesto that called "on the governments of the world to encourage women everywhere to take a more conscious part in national and international affairs, and on women to come forward and share in the work of peace and reconstruction as they did in the war and resistance."[2] She also sat through so many impassioned, mind-numbing speeches on just the rules of procedure alone that she actually considered taking her knitting along so she could feel like something worthwhile was happening.

She was assigned to Committee III, which addressed humanitarian, social, and cultural matters and whose work was expected to be relatively noncontroversial. However, this committee actually became the stage for a high drama regarding the world's refugees, a drama that pitted the United States' political philosophies against Russia's, and proved once again the mettle of America's former First Lady. She wrote in her journal: "A new type of political refugee is appearing . . . people who have been against the present governments and if they stay at home or go home will probably be killed." She knew her topic well: In early 1947 more than one million refugees were living in makeshift camps—most from Communist countries. United Nations delegates representing Russia held a simple—if brutal—belief that the refugee question had no place in international conversation because, after all, there are only two kinds of refugees: those who are willing to be repatriated and those who are traitors and deserve no sympathy.

In a final tension-filled showdown before the entire assembly, Eleanor eloquently represented the views of the majority of her colleagues when she debated the refugee question against Andrei Vishinsky, the head of the Russian delegation. She spoke extemporaneously, defending the rights of the world's citizens to hear and to speak both good and bad about governments, and she defended the underlying philosophy that puts the rights of humans first in any political debate. The United Nations' most important duty, she said, was to focus on that which gives greater freedom to humans—not governments. The Soviet amendments (which, in essence, represented a license to kill "traitorous" refugees) were soundly defeated within the assembly, and Eleanor wryly noted to one friend back in America: "I'm rather old to be carrying on this fight!"[3]

In fact, the best was yet to come. In the extemporaneous debate against her Soviet nemesis, Eleanor had articulated the basic human rights which American allies had just wrestled back from Nazism and fascism, and she so clearly personified the cause of respect for human dignity that she immediately was asked to serve on what was called the "nuclear" commission on human rights for the United Nations. This was the committee that would produce the eighteen-nation Human Rights Commission, which, in turn, produced "a Magna Charta for humankind." The Universal Declaration of Human Rights was a hard-fought document, and as chairman of the commission, Eleanor Roosevelt once again was in the middle of the fight.

The commission began in January 1947, and early, lengthy discussions on philosophies ranging from Thomas Aquinas to Confucius soon revealed two prominent schools of thought among the delegates. The question "Whose rights are more important, the individual's or the nation's?" produced *constant* disagreements. In addition, members of the Soviet delegation were quick to manipulate the commission's decisions as a way of embarrassing the American government within the international community. In light of its growing frustration with Russia and the postwar swing to the political right, the United States Congress became increasingly wary of any document Eleanor's commission might produce. Perhaps the most important reason for the growing United States disenchantment, however, is that Eleanor Roosevelt's efforts could actually produce a document that might be used against the United States itself and its treatment of African Americans. Southern politicians were absolutely opposed to any such treatise.

Still, Eleanor continued to help frame the document through the difficult process until on June 18, 1948, the Human Rights Commission adopted a final draft. In December the United Nations General Assembly approved and adopted the declaration, which became a living document that found its way into many constitutions, is cited often in domestic court decisions throughout the world, and is the customary law of most nations. It clearly entered the ethical conscience of humankind.

After reading the document in braille, Helen Keller wrote: "My soul stood erect, exultant, envisioning a new world where the light of justice for every individual will be unclouded." Pope John XXIII, in one encyclical, described the declaration as both "an act of highest importance" and an "important step on the path towards the juridical-political organization of the world community."[4] In 1962 President Kennedy nominated Eleanor Roosevelt for the Nobel Peace Prize, but she did not win. However, the United Nations awarded her posthumously its first Human Rights Prize.

In 1958 she wrote:

> Where, after all, do universal human rights begin? In small places, close to home—so close and so small that they cannot be seen on any maps of the world. Yet they *are* the world of the individual persons; the neighborhood he lives in; the school or college he attends; the factory, farm or office where he works. Such are the places where every man, woman and child seeks equal justice, equal opportunity, equal dignity without discrimination. Unless these rights have meaning there, they have little meaning anywhere. Without concerned citizen action to uphold them close to home, we shall look in vain for progress in the larger world.[5]

While her work on the universal document of human rights was her greatest contribution to the world, Eleanor Roosevelt's best contribution to America was probably her tireless efforts during World War II. If Franklin Roosevelt ever suffered indigestion after dinner, Eleanor—with her overwhelming sense of duty and inability to know *when* to put issues aside—was the likely cause. The joke among the family was that Franklin's daily prayer was painfully simple: "O God, please let Eleanor get tired today." But Eleanor was as energetic and as outspoken on this topic as any.

As early as in a speech in 1923, she said she felt women had an obligation to treat international peace as a personal crusade. She asked her audience, "Cannot the women rise to this great opportunity and work now, and not have the double horror if another war comes of losing their loved ones, and knowing that they lifted no finger when they might have worked hard?"

As Hitler's aggression increased and her husband tried with some success to thwart the Nazi leader through negotiations, Eleanor said, "No one could be objective about a war who had ever seen the results of one. I am greatly relieved that we haven't a war going on this minute. On the other hand it seems to me a very unsatisfactory peace and I am afraid it is not permanent." As the Nazi problems continued and her husband sought to assist European countries with supplies and money (but not troops), Eleanor often had to answer questions in public about his action. In a speech to the New York Youth Congress she said, "You don't want to go to war. I don't want to go to war. But war may come to us."[6]

When Japanese bombers attacked Pearl Harbor on December 7, 1941, Eleanor Roosevelt in her capacity as assistant director of the Office of Civilian Defense flew immediately to the West Coast even though officials in that region were anticipating another attack. To her friend Joseph Lash, she wrote: "One thing among many others I've learned, if we have trouble anywhere I must go because it does seem to calm people down."[7]

At the outbreak of the war, Eleanor floundered for a bit in search of the right place to direct her efforts. She found it in the American GI, and he became her cause as surely as she represented every American mother who sent a son or husband overseas. In fact, all four of Eleanor's boys as well as her son-in-law were in the military—a point that raised anxiety considerably from time to time in the White House. While stateside she visited the GIs—both white and black—on their bases, at Union Station, and even at the airport before they departed for Europe or the South Pacific.

She hated the Japanese relocation camps created by the American government and felt powerless in the face of them. But for the GIs she represented someone who was listening and who could help. She personally answered every letter she received from a member of the military. She rewrote FDR's letter of condolence into a kinder, gentler version. She worried that black soldiers were getting more dangerous assignments than white soldiers, and she visited lots of GIs recuperating in Washington hospitals.

Eleanor became the first First Lady to fly the Atlantic in October 1942 when she flew to England to inspect American Red Cross units, check on volunteer organizations, see bombed-out sections of London, visit with military units, and, of course, tend the wounded. She was known for speaking to each man in the infirmary, asking if he needed anything. Could she write to his family? Was there anyone special he wanted her to contact? Was his equipment adequate? She congratulated and thanked them for all their efforts. She made sure the best seats at a USO show were reserved for the GIs and *not* the top brass. And through it all she confided to her closest friends that she simply felt she wasn't doing very much at all that was useful in the war effort. Irony prevailed in the life of Eleanor Roosevelt.

In May 1943, as a special delegate for the American Red Cross, she took off for an extended, grueling trip to the South Pacific, where she personally saw more than 400,000 GIs and visited Guadalcanal just hours after it was bombed by Japan. She stopped in Australia, New Zealand, and seemingly any small island where American men might be stationed.

During the Normandy invasion, Eleanor Roosevelt—like the rest of America—said she hoped for a quick end to the war. Then she added, "It is not enough to win the fight. We must win *that for which we fight*—the triumph of all people who believe that the people of this world are worthy of freedom."[8] While her husband did not live to see his nation restored to peace, Eleanor knew he believed the greatest security for the United States would come with its involvement in an international organization fundamentally dedicated to justice and peace. For more than fifteen years after FDR's death, Eleanor Roosevelt continued to promote her favorite issues of human dignity and peace through her syndicated column *My Day:*

> March 9, 1955: One of the real gifts that brings you riches, I think, is the power of appreciation. If you can enjoy the blue sky, the beauty of the fresh snow, or the first green of spring, if you can hear music and have it leave a song in your heart, if you can see a picture and take away something that is real and vital to dream about for days, then you have the ability to get joy out of your surroundings. That kind of appreciation is perhaps more valuable than some more tangible kinds of riches.

> August 25, 1954: The sermon in our church on last Sunday dealt with the admonition to love one another, and the misunderstandings

which might arise over the question of forgiveness and how often that forgiveness should be granted. In thinking it over afterwards, it seemed to me that in the world today it is sometimes rather difficult to follow the spirit and the teachings of Christ.

I do not think I really hate anyone in the world, but I must say that sometimes I find it puzzling to separate the sin which is being committed from the sinner. I am sure of one thing, however. If in any way we can keep from war during the next few years, that achievement certainly will be one of the things that church people will feel has helped them to achieve the ideals of their religions. For war certainly intensifies all the hatreds between people.

Some people I know feel that the strain today—the possibility of atomic war—is unbearable. But that, I think, is really a challenge to those of us who believe that God will not destroy willingly. Only if we, through our blindness, fail to carry out His will as we have in the past, and perhaps will again, will we (not God) achieve destruction.

That knowledge should make us work harder than we have ever worked to build a better world. . . . I am convinced, however, that one of the essential steps that must be taken throughout the world is for individuals to try to set their own houses in order, to get rid of feelings of hate and to try to develop charity and understanding in the circles that they individually touch.

February 6, 1958: The theme of this World Day of Prayer is "The Bread of Life," and this is the day when throughout the world many peoples will repeat the prophecy of Isaiah: "He shall judge between nations, He shall decide from many peoples; and they shall beat their swords into ploughshares, and their spears into pruning hooks; nation shall not lift sword against nation, neither shall they learn war any more."

Perhaps the time has come when the prophecy shall come to mean something real to the peoples of the earth, who are now capable of self-destruction and therefore need inspiration and intelligence to keep them from committing suicide. Regardless of their religion, people throughout the world are thinking along the same lines.

Martha Washington

When Martha Washington served as a compassionate nurse to the patriots who fought in the Revolutionary War, she couldn't have known that she represented millions of future American women who, like herself, would watch their husbands and sons go into battle. While American colonists struggled against British tyranny in the mid-1770s, George Washington said their "lordly masters in Great Britain" would be satisfied with nothing less than the deprecation of American freedom. Something had to be done to "maintain the liberty which we have derived from our ancestors," he wrote. "But the manner of doing it to answer the purpose effectually is the point in question. That no man should scruple or hesitate to use arms in defense of so valuable a blessing, on which all the good and evil of life depend is clearly my opinion."

These were not the words of a man eager for blood. It was the writing of one who knew the fight was inevitable and who'd been told by many he was not just the obvious leader, he was the *only* leader who could keep the other generals' egos in order, who drew the respect of the newly formed Continental Congress, and who was best prepared to shape a ragtag volunteer army into a disciplined, effective force. Like her husband, Martha was not reckless in her claims for patriots' freedom. In fact, she had considered herself a British subject until the Boston Massacre in 1770. But as the chasm widened between the patriots and the British, both George and Martha Washington accepted that war was undesired but inevitable.

In August 1774 Mount Vernon visitor Edmund Pendleton addressed with Martha the possibility of war. "She talked like a Spartan mother to her son on going to battle. 'I hope you will all stand firm—I know George will,' she said. When we set off in the morning, she stood in the door and cheered us with good words. 'God be with you gentlemen.' "[9]

The following summer, in June 1775, Washington became commander of all continental forces and was headquartered in Cambridge, Massachusetts. By October his officers learned of a British plan to capture Martha and burn Mount Vernon. When George Mason rushed to her home to take her to safety, she refused at first. However, when a British transport was sighted off the Mount Vernon landing, she went with Mason but refused to be away from her home for more than one night. In response to this scare, General Washington preferred to have his wife with him each winter at camp.

For her part, Martha was so dedicated to the soldiers who served her husband that she usually stayed very busy at camp, spending her time treating illness, sharing delicacies from Mount Vernon, and recruiting other women to help her care for the men. Soldiers' letters and journals reveal that her presence, her constant concern for their welfare, and her inquiries about their families back home made camp life—even the despicable, deadly Valley Forge—more bearable. One matron visiting the camp wrote:

> I was never so ashamed in my life. [We] . . . thought we would visit Lady Washington, and as she was said to be so grand a lady, we thought we must put on our best bibs and bands. So we dressed ourselves in our most elegant ruffles and silks, and were introduced to her ladyship. And don't you think we found her knitting and with a specked [checked] apron on! She received us very graciously, but after the compliments were over, she resumed her knitting. . . . She seems very wise in experience, kind-hearted and winning all her ways. She talked much of the poor soldiers, especially the sick ones. Her heart seems to be full of compassion for them. . . .[10]

Martha also knew extensive details of her husband's military strategies because he confided in her constantly, and she did clerical work for him.

> I never in my life knew a woman so busy from early morning until late at night as was Lady Washington, providing comforts for the sick soldiers," reported one of the other military wives from Valley Forge. "Everyday, excepting Sunday, the wives of the officers in camp, and sometimes other women, were invited . . . to assist her in knitting socks, patching garments, and make shirts for the poor soldiers, when materials could be procured. Every fair day she might be seen, with basket in hand, and with a single attendant, going among the huts seeking the keenest and most needy sufferer, and giving all the comforts to him in her power.[11]

When an Englishman touring the United States after the Revolution visited Mount Vernon in 1785, he was stunned by her pride in the troops and her knowledge of military affairs.

> It's astonishing with what raptures Mrs. Washington spoke about the discipline of the army, the excellent order they were in, superior to any troops she said upon the face of the earth towards the close of the war; even the English acknowledge it, she said. What pleasure she took in the sound of the fifes and drums, preferring it to any music that was ever heard; and then to see them reviewed a week or two before the men were disbanded, when they were all well clothed was, she said, a most heavenly sight. . . .[12]

Aiding the Cause

Martha Washington also stood as a grand example for future First Ladies. Like Martha, Mary Lincoln, Carrie Harrison, Lucy Hayes, Margaret Taylor, Eleanor Roosevelt, Edith Wilson, Barbara Bush, Hillary Clinton, and Pat Nixon visited or tended men injured in war. Julia Grant became so sympathetic to the soldiers, her husband ordered her to stop nursing because she brought back to his headquarters too many requests for discharge from the Union soldiers. Mary Lincoln genuinely enjoyed nursing the soldiers. She visited the hospitals regularly, handing out fresh fruits, treating soldiers to bouquets of fresh flowers, and writing letters for soldiers to their families back home. She donated generously to the military hospital wards, shipped fresh bread from the White House, and distributed citrus fruits to prevent scurvy.

Edith Wilson

As part of her efforts to economize and help the American cause during World War I, Edith Wilson let twenty sheep graze on the White House lawn, and sold their wool to raise money for the Red Cross and the

Salvation Army. During the day she sewed hundreds of items for soldiers, including pajamas, pillowcases, and blankets. At night she decoded messages for her husband. She appeared with Mary Pickford and Charlie Chaplin to promote war bonds, and she personally responded to mail from soldiers' mothers. Edith christened sea transports, ships, and destroyers.

Edith also traveled with her husband to Paris, where she visited wounded soldiers. "The room seemed to be turning upside down and through a mist I saw human forms with faces so distorted and mutilated that the place seemed an inferno," she wrote in her memoirs. In efforts to support the cause, future First Lady Lou Hoover assumed leadership in handling Washington's housing shortage which was brought on by an influx of war workers. Former First Lady Lucretia Garfield, then eighty-five and living in Pasadena, volunteered daily for her local Red Cross committee, and former First Lady Frances Cleveland Preston became director of the National Security League's Speakers' Bureau, a role she used to travel the country winning support for American troops.

Dolley Madison

One of the most memorable events in American history and one of the defining moments of the War of 1812 happened on August 24, 1814, at the White House. President James Madison left the Executive Mansion to be with American troops at Bladensberg while Dolley stayed behind to tend to duties. Anticipating her husband would return with some military leaders, she went to the roof with binoculars to look for him. To her horror, she saw not her husband but panic-stricken residents fleeing with what possessions they could grab on the run.

The British were coming.

As the day passed, Washington's mayor three times asked Dolley to evacuate. Despite the sounds of British cannon in the background and despite rumors that British generals hoped to kidnap Dolley, she felt that abandoning her post was inexcusable. She just *wished* she had a row of cannon herself to use against the enemy, she later wrote.

When she received word from Madison himself, she agreed to leave but not before she gave an order that would be one of the most historic gestures of any First Lady. She ordered her guards to slice Gilbert Stuart's portrait of George Washington from its frame. She gathered other important national documents, then disguised herself as a farmer's wife before fleeing with a bodyguard.

The British set fire to the White House, leaving a gutted shell. Dolley sought shelter from one tavernkeeper's wife, who rudely evicted her, saying, "Mis' Madison, if that's you, come down and go out. Your husband has got mine out fighting and, damn you, you shan't stay in my house, so get out!"[13]

Dolley Madison returned to Washington days later under great celebration and dedicated herself to rebuilding what the British had destroyed. The war ended February 15, 1815, and Dolley was lauded as a genuine war hero.

The Charming Diplomat

We have no way of knowing, of course, just how many bridges our First Ladies built to foreign countries, how many misunderstandings they diffused, or how many fights they prevented. However, there are many examples of moments when the grace and charm, cunning and wit of a First Lady were uniquely effective. For instance, Carrie Harrison, Lady Bird Johnson, and Grace Coolidge were known for balancing and even compensating for their husbands' personal styles—Ben Harrison with his austere and sometimes humorless posture, Lyndon Johnson with his take-no-prisoners determination, and Calvin Coolidge with his remarkably inept social skills.

In the foreign affairs department, First Ladies have been especially effective.

When she visited France in August 1861, Mary Lincoln charmed her host with her fluent French, and some historians credit her with France's decision to remain neutral—rather than support the Confederacy—during the Civil War.

Jackie Kennedy so charmed the French during a visit with her husband that she commanded greater attention at some of the events than he did. She amazed French leaders, including President Charles de Gaulle, with her knowledge of French history, theater, and literature. She even served as an interpreter for her husband and de Gaulle.

At what seemed the height of the cold war—when President Kennedy and Soviet President Nikita Khrushchev could not reach an amicable agreement—Jackie charmed the Russian leader during a state dinner. On a goodwill trip to Europe she became the first First Lady to be received by a pope, and she also met privately with Italian president Giovanni Gronchi, the first time a First Lady met with a European leader who was democratically elected. Jackie also smoothed over diplomatic strains between the United States and India when she visited that nation as First Lady. She managed this in large part by demonstrating not just a sophisticated knowledge of India's customs, but also a willingness and ability to practice them—from her first salutation when she stepped off the plane to her poignant visit at the grave of Mahatma Gandhi.

In early 1972 Patricia Nixon became the first First Lady to travel to Africa. She went there on an eight-day trip to visit Liberia, Ghana, and the Ivory Coast. In Liberia she received a nineteen-gun salute typically reserved for heads of government. She reviewed Liberia's honor guard and met with President William R. Tolbert, Jr., for diplomatic talks. Before Pat's departure, Liberia awarded her its highest honor, the Grand Cordon of the Most Venerable Order of Knighthood. In the Ivory Coast, a quarter of a million residents met her and cheered *"Vive Madame Nixon!"* as her car headed toward the capital.

Rosalynn Carter

Just six months after she became the First Lady, Rosalynn Carter served as her husband's official envoy to Latin America. She visited Jamaica, Costa Rica, Ecuador, Peru, Brazil, Colombia, and Venezuela. Each visit followed a similar pattern: She delivered a brief statement on America's policy toward the nation and addressed her husband's concern for human rights and nuclear weaponry. The topics she discussed with the nations' leaders ranged from demilitarization and arms reduction to beef exports and nuclear energy. In Peru she even mediated a dispute with Ecuador over arms buildup.

When one United States reporter questioned her validity as an American representative and pointed out that she was neither elected nor Senate-appointed, Rosalynn fired back, "I am the person closest to the president of the United States, and if I can explain his policies and let the people of Latin America know of his great interest and friendship, I intend to do so!" Less than a week after she returned home, Rosalynn received a seventy-four percent approval rating for her role as ambassador.

When the Camp David summit began in September 1978 between Egyptian president Anwar Sadat and Israeli prime minister Menachem Begin, Jimmy and Rosalynn Carter were well aware of two significant political facts about the event: 1) Given the long-standing hatred between the two countries and its potential for permanent damage to international peace, some effort had to be made to resolve the conflict; 2) While putting the two leaders together seemed the best plan, no one in the American government thought it could work—no one except Jimmy and Rosalynn Carter.

Throughout the intense twelve days of emotional, often bitter negotiations between the two enemies, Rosalynn was her husband's full partner. Not only did she coordinate the overwhelming logistics involved in feeding and housing the hundred people on the grounds, she also served as her husband's adviser and spent a fair amount of time with both Sadat and Begin. Rosalynn kept an extremely detailed journal of the events, a diary that eventually totaled two hundred typed pages.

She also coordinated an international "call to prayer" the first day of the summit in which she released a carefully worded prayer for peace that would be acceptable to Christian, Muslim, and Jew: "After four years, despite vast human efforts, the Holy Land does not yet enjoy the blessings of peace. Conscious of the grave issues which face us, we place our trust in the God of our fathers, from whom we seek wisdom and guidance. As we meet here at Camp David, we ask people of all faiths to pray with us that peace and justice may result from these deliberations."

The peace accord that Jimmy Carter negotiated was hard fought for, and right up until the very last minute, no one was certain America's efforts would prove fruitful. Rosalynn had returned to Washington to attend to some White House duties when she got word that after twelve extremely difficult days an accord would be signed. She broke down and cried. "It was done," she wrote. "The impossible had been made possible. Through all the hard work and despite all the worry, the misery and the ups and downs, it was done. A miracle? Yes, for anyone who had been there and seen the obstacles and the hard feelings and adamant positions—it was a miracle."[14] Sadat and Begin shared the Nobel Peace Prize for the accord. Because of a long-standing policy of the Nobel committee that the prize should not be shared by more than two people, Jimmy Carter was not named.

Edith Roosevelt

On February 8, 1904, Japan attacked Port Arthur in Russian-held Manchuria, and while the news item meant virtually nothing to Americans, America's president knew it meant possible war for the two nations, and the United States as well. In January 1904 Edith Roosevelt became secretly enmeshed in a long series of delicate diplomatic maneuvers that helped bring leaders of both nations together to the negotiation table with her husband.

She and her husband had a private meeting in the White House with British diplomat Cecil Spring-Rice, who spoke as an unofficial adviser on the matter. Russia wanted to occupy all of Japan, he reported. Japan's attack on Port Arthur was a warning against Russian aggression. The most hideous account, however, was that Russian soldiers attacked their own citizens, who took to the streets in a nonviolent protest—a protest against Japan. "His tales of Russia were such as to make one feel that rebellion against such a government is a holy war," Edith wrote.

Roosevelt wanted continual reports from Spring-Rice, but, because of glitches with the British government was not able to correspond with him directly. So Edith did, and the information she collected for her husband for nearly a year aided his eventual plans to negotiate peace and his immediate plans "to keep American in trim, so that fighting her shall be too expensive and dangerous a task to likely be undertaken by anybody."

On Saturday, August 5, 1905, peace emissaries from Russia and Japan boarded the *Mayflower* to join Teddy Roosevelt in a series of talks that lasted less than four hours but produced the outline of a peace agreement between the two nations. Congratulations to Roosevelt poured in from around the globe: Tsar Nicholas, Kaiser Wilhelm, King Edward VII, the Archbishop of Canterbury, and the international head of the Salvation Army. Press all over the world saluted Roosevelt's achievements with such lavish words as these: "A master of diplomacy such as does not otherwise exist. He held the mandate of the civilized world, and he made his task epochal." "One is so frequently disappointed by one's heroes," said a Russian diplomat to an American reporter. "But your President is so real and vital and full of magnetism."[15]

Mrs. Roosevelt's contribution—her valuable advice to her husband as he used her for a sounding board and her secret correspondence with Spring-Rice—was not fully understood or acknowledged for decades. Together Teddy and Edith Roosevelt decided they would not keep the $40,000 awarded with the Nobel Prize. The president wired Norway and suggested the money be used to establish an industrial peace committee, created to develop more equitable relationships between workers and corporate management.

Julia Grant

Not long before General Grant's final move to capture Richmond, his wife, Julia, attended him in camp. Late one afternoon she walked through his office, where she found him in light conversation with General Ord.

General Grant called her to them. "See here, Mrs. Grant, what do you think of this," he asked. "Ord has been across the lines on a flag of truce and brings a suggestion that terms of peace may be reached through you, and a suggestion of an interchange of social visits between you and Mrs. Longstreet and others when the subject of peace may be discussed, and you ladies may become the mediums of peace."

"Oh! How enchanting, how thrilling!" she exclaimed. "Oh, Ulys, I may go, may I not?"

But the general only smiled at her enthusiasm and said, "No, I think not."

"Yes, I must," she said. "Do say yes. I so much wish to go. Do let me go."

But Grant replied gently that he did not feel sure he could trust her because she might propose some policy President Lincoln could not sanction. "No, that would never do," he said.

Throughout most of her memoirs, Julia Grant heaps the sweetest of praise upon her husband—an account almost in total contrast to that of more objective historians—but in her account of this exchange she reveals a rare moment of total disgust with the man.

"I replied to this: 'Oh, nonsense. Do not talk so, but let me go. . . . I must go. I will. Do say I may go.' But General Grant grew very earnest now and said: 'No, you must not. It is simply absurd. The men have fought this war, and the men will finish it.'

"I urged no more, knowing it was final, and I was silent, indignant and disappointed."[16]

Abigail Adams

Fate turned John Adams's heart to ice on November 30, 1800, the day he lost his son Charles to alcoholism and the very same day he lost the presidency to Thomas Jefferson, who had been his friend for thirty years and his own vice president for four. Adams was unable to accept the defeat with grace or dignity. While the democracy was too young to claim an inaugural tradition, President Washington in 1796 had established the courteous precedent of riding with Adams to the Capitol, listening to his speech, and congratulating him when he took the oath of office. Washington's gesture was noted by national leaders, but playing a role in his successor's inauguration was beyond Adams's magnanimity. Before sunrise on March 4, 1801, John Adams rode away from Washington, D.C., and never visited it again. For the rest of his life Adams's bitterness and anguish seemed to be focused on one man.

To make matters worse, Jefferson's administration further insulted John and Abigail Adams by throwing a political blow to their son, John Quincy Adams, who had distinguished himself in foreign service. This was a personal tragedy considering Thomas Jefferson and John Adams stood shoulder to shoulder in the difficult, arduous process that created the Declaration of Independence and birthed a nation in 1776. Prior to this bitter misunderstanding between the two men, Abigail had developed her own friendship with Jefferson, considered him "one of the choice ones of the earth," and exchanged letters with him, discussing literature, theater, and even gossip. All correspondence between Jefferson and either John or Abigail ended abruptly when the political differences surfaced.

In 1804, however, when she learned Jefferson suffered the death of his youngest daughter (Maria, whose nickname was Polly), Abigail wrote an endearing letter expressing both her sympathy for the president's family and her favorite memories of the young woman. Abigail cared for Polly abroad when Jefferson and the Adamses were stationed there in government appointments. With that letter, Thomas Jefferson and Abigail Adams both decided to put their anger aside and reclaim peace. Each knew the cost of war. Each knew the anguish of losing children. Those were life's most bitter hours. They knew they would never agree on the issues that separated them, but wasting time on personal feuding must have seemed secondary in light of those extreme experiences of human suffering.

He responded to her letter with language of respect and warmth: "Dear Madam, I have received duly the honor of your letter, and am now to return you thanks for your condescension in having taken the first step for settling a correspondence which I so much desired. . . ."

Abigail ended her first letter to him as one "who once took pleasure in subscribing Herself your Friend." Jefferson responded to this point directly: "The friendship with which you honored me has ever been valued and fully reciprocated." Unfortunately, the friendship with John Adams was not repairable. For less than a year, however, Abigail and President Jefferson explored through correspondence the painful issues that separated them and together they constructed a bridge back to each other.

Abigail—who had written to Jefferson in confidence—eventually turned all her letters over to her husband. Brought together as younger men by mutual dedication to the concept of democracy, then torn apart by political bitterness that would be inherent to the system they helped create, Jefferson and Adams were ultimately united by death. On July 4, 1826, in one of the most remarkable and ironic footnotes in American history, John Adams and

Thomas Jefferson died within hours of each other and on the fiftieth anniversary of the signing of the Declaration of Independence. Among the last surviving signers, Adams knew his death was imminent but didn't know his colleague had already died when he whispered, "Jefferson still lives."[17]

Lou Hoover and the Boxer Rebellion

In the early months of 1900, in the northern region of China, a group of antiforeigner Chinese zealots grew in its determination and power to eradicate any outside influence. These militants called themselves "I-ho-ch'uan," which translates as "righteous harmonious fists." However, the threatened foreigners—missionaries, teachers, businessmen—called them simply "the Boxers." They swept through regions massacring Chinese Christians (sometimes burning them alive), setting fire to anything identified as Western property, as well as missionary churches, and threatening to kill every foreigner in the entire country. France, Britain, and America all had growing cultural, political, and religious influence there.

By June 1900 the home of Herbert and Lou Hoover—they already had been in China about eighteen months on one of their extremely lucrative mining expeditions—came under siege as the Boxers attacked the northern city of Tientsin. Their home was located within a foreign settlement that battled desperately for survival: 400 male civilians, 300 women and children, and about 2,500 foreign soldiers confronted 5,000 trained Chinese soldiers and 25,000 angry Boxers. During the worst of the siege, the women and children huddled in the spacious cellar of the settlement's large city hall. Lou Hoover did not join them though. Carrying a Mauser automatic .38-caliber pistol, Lou managed a dairy herd (essential for survival during the siege), bicycled throughout the village on errands, and volunteered very long hours as a nurse in the hospital. She was a good shot with her revolver but never fired it during the siege.

To her husband's annoyance, Lou refused to leave the settlement when the first groups of women and children were sent away during a break in the battle in early July. According to Hoover biographer George Nash: "One day a shell burst in the yard of the Hoover home. Instead of prudently seeking shelter at once behind a wall, Lou went to investigate where it had landed. A moment later a second shell crashed on the nearby street. Since the Chinese gunners were known to fire three missiles at a target in a row, another could be expected within seconds. It came—and exploded inside the Hoover house at the foot of the stairs. In a nearby room Palmer discovered Mrs. Hoover amidst the dust calmly playing solitaire." (Frederick Palmer was a former war correspondent who became a lifelong friend of the Hoovers.)[18]

Through their superstition, patriotism, and stunning fanaticism, the Boxers practiced magic rituals and asserted their powers to fly, to rise from the dead, and to resist the penetration of Western bullets. Despite Lou's calm response to her circumstances, the Boxers' influence on the country was one of total chaos. After the grisly month-long battle in Tientsin that left thousands of Chinese bodies floating down the nearby Peiho River—the Chinese soldiers and Boxer militants were fighting each other while fighting the foreigners—came a climax when more than 5,500 foreign troops, including American marines and Japanese soldiers, stormed the Boxer stronghold. One of their guides was the future president, who knew the terrain well as a result of regular horseback rides with Lou.

The units successfully disbanded the Boxers, and the twenty-day ordeal—which dropped thousands of shells on the settlement, leveled buildings, and sparked revenge in the form of looting, rape, and murder—was over.

So what can one woman do to prevent war? Eleanor answered her own question with her tireless service to the United Nations and her prolific writings, including the December 20, 1961 *My Day* column:

> To the women and the men who are asking themselves "What can I do as an individual?" my answer is this: Take a more active interest in your government, have a say in who is nominated for political office, work for these candidates and keep in close touch with them if they are elected.
>
> If our objective is to do away with the causes of war, build up the United Nations and give the UN more control over the weapons of total destruction, we should urge that world law be developed so that people's grievances can be heard promptly and judiciously settled.

> We should begin in our own environment and in our own community as far as possible to build a peace-loving attitude and learn to discipline ourselves to accept, in the small things of our lives, mediation and arbitration . . . we can work to gain greater understanding of other people and to try to present to the people of the world the values of our own beliefs. We can do this by demonstrating our conviction that human life is worth preserving and that we are willing to help others to enjoy benefits of our civilization just as we have enjoyed it.

Though it is superficially associated with lily-white serenity and the attainment of inner tranquility, *peace* is a rather intense concept, especially as reflected in the lives of our First Ladies. We hear the expression "Peace like a river" and may think of a gentle stream, when it could also be white-water rapids if Eleanor Roosevelt's or Rosalynn Carter's life is considered. In scripture peace is inevitably linked to strength, righteousness, and holiness. For the actions of our First Ladies it also is linked to determination, mercy, and human dignity.

Echoes of This Beatitude in the Bible

Psalm 122:6–9: "Pray for the peace of Jerusalem: 'May those who love you be secure. May there be peace within your walls and security within your citadels.' For the sake of my brothers and friends, I will say, 'Peace be within you.' For the sake of the house of the Lord, our God, I will seek your prosperity."

Luke 2:14: "Glory to God in the highest, and peace to men on whom his favor rests."

Psalm 4:8: "I will lie down and sleep in peace, for you alone, O Lord, make me dwell in safety."

John 14:27: "Peace I leave with you; my peace I give you. I do not give to you as the world gives. Do not let your hearts be troubled and do not be afraid."

Psalm 29:11: "The Lord gives strength to his people; the Lord bless his people with peace."

Philippians 4:7: "And the peace of God, which transcends all understanding, will guard your hearts and your minds in Christ Jesus."

Psalm 85:10: "Love and faithfulness meet together; righteousness and peace kiss each other."

Hebrews 12:14: "Make every effort to live in peace with all men and to be holy; without holiness no one will see the Lord."

Jude 1:2: "Mercy, peace and love be yours in abundance."

I Corinthians 14:33: "For God is not a God of disorder but of peace. . . ."

Romans 8:6: "The mind of sinful man is death, but the mind controlled by the Spirit is life and peace. . . ."

First Lady Quotables

"The difficulties and distresses to which we have been exposed during the war must now be forgotten. We must endeavor to let our ways be the way of pleasantness and all our paths Peace."

—Martha Washington

"I think that if the atomic bomb did nothing more, it scared the people to the point where they realized that either they must do something about preventing war or there is a chance that there might be a morning when we would not wake up."

—Eleanor Roosevelt

"I became so absorbed in these poor fellows, the wounded, the sick and the dying, I could think of nothing else."

—Julia Grant

"Will we ever awaken from this hideous nightmare?"

—Mary Lincoln on the Civil War

"We know that our men . . . have many trying hours ahead. Hours in which we will . . . be restless and unnerved. . . . And yet if we ask our fighting men what they would have us do, they would tell us 'remaining as cheerful and busy as possible.' So let's have faith . . . and work a little harder than ever before. . . ."

—Mamie Eisenhower on the launch of the D-day invasion

"Harry always placed high value on the life of every single American boy. If the war with Japan had been allowed to continue, it would have claimed the lives of perhaps a quarter million American soldiers, and twice that number would have been maimed for life. It's difficult to calculate the number of Japanese lives that would have been lost . . . as many or more, undoubtedly, as died at Hiroshima and Nagasaki. So the atom bomb was the lesser weapon, although it's hard to look at it that way."

—Bess Truman on her husband's decision to use the atomic bomb

"The year of 1775, was the eighth year of my age. . . . For the space of twelve months my mother, with her infant children, dwelt liable every hour of the day and of the night to be butchered in cold blood—of being consumed with them all in a conflagration, kindled by a torch in the same hands which, on the Seventeenth of June, lighted the fires of Charlestown. I saw with my own eyes those fires from Penn's Hill, and witnessed the tears of my mother and mingled with them my own at the fall of Warren, a dear friend of my father, and a beloved physician to me. . . . Before, there had been only strife and bickerings with the mother country; occasionally, an humble remonstrance was laid at the foot of the throne, but now Americans were rebels, rebels in arms, who, as Franklin wittily put it, 'must all hang together or all hang separately.' "

—John Quincy Adams

Photo on page 174:

Eleanor Roosevelt examines the Universal Declaration of Human Rights, a statement on the basic rights of every person in the world. It was her greatest gift to humankind.

Photo courtesy of the Franklin D. Roosevelt Library

Blessed are those who
are persecuted because
of righteousness,
for theirs is the
kingdom of heaven.

Rachel Jackson

Chapter Eight

Blessed are those who are persecuted because of righteousness, for theirs is the kingdom of heaven.

The Persecuted First Ladies

I sometimes think we should change our concept of the world's oldest profession. Instead of prostitution, I would cast my ballot for persecution. In the beginning there was Adam and Eve, whose painful spiritual illumination—they came to know both good and evil—forced them with a naked, powerful push right out of the garden of perfection. Theologically, this couple represents spiritual awakening regarding human nature and the human experience, which, of course, are both good and evil. You simply cannot reach emotional adulthood without having been chased from the garden yourself.

And on their heels came Cain and Abel. One tended the soil. The other tended the animals. One found favor in the sight of God. The other became a persecutor, killing his brother with such violence that the dead man's blood cried out to God from beneath the soil. *Paradox* is the first and last word to describe human spirituality, and that paradox is never more poignant, tragic, or accurate than in this portrait of the first humans, an image that places what gives life next to what steals it.

Persecution steals life, and persecution in the name of any deity certainly is among the greatest evils related to our humanness. It is the act of deliberately throwing chaos upon excellence or innocence, and it is like watching a hungry rattlesnake happen upon an abandoned kitten in that it becomes easy prey. Persecution's greatest victim is human dignity, and ultimately it pulls every last one of us right out of the Garden of Eden.

Rachel Jackson

Theirs was a love story quite fitting for the adventurous and dangerous American frontier of 1790: An impulsive, handsome young lawyer rescues a distressed woman from her abusive husband and delivers her back to the safety of her family. He falls in love with this kind, vivacious, and it must be noted—deeply religious—woman. His affection brings life back to her desolate soul, and they dedicate themselves to each other with such passion and strength, it's hard to imagine anything except a very happy ending.

But the end was cruel and devastating for Rachel and Andrew Jackson, and it offered bitter evidence that a political attack launched in the name of Jesus could, in fact, be deadly for both body and spirit.

When they got married, each one unwittingly brought to the union an element that would cause great suffering to the other. Rachel Donelson Robards brought the reputation of a ruined woman, a predilection toward piety that could be a bit much at times—though it never seemed to bother her second husband—and a strong need for privacy.

Andrew Jackson brought with him a flair and love for public leadership, a quick temper, and a reputation for being absolutely thorough in his loyalties, and there was nothing subtle about his loyalty to Rachel. Even before he admitted to her he was in love with her, he threatened her first husband, Lewis Robards, by saying he would cut off Robards's ears if he ever went near Rachel again. Robards apparently believed him, because he left Rachel alone, moved away, and sent back word that he filed for divorce.

For her part, Rachel Robards was self-preserving enough to get out of an emotionally and physically abusive marriage (she tried reconciliation twice), but even at the tender age of twenty-three, she was prepared to live the rest of her life as permanently separated from her husband because no woman of decent standing was divorced in 1790 in America. When Jackson gave her the mortifying news that her husband had filed for divorce on grounds she deserted him, she said, "I expected him to kill me but this is worse."[1]

If Rachel had not understood Jackson's affection toward her up to this point, he made certain she understood it now. The two were married in the fall of 1791. Each one was twenty-four years old. Each one was thoroughly devoted to the other. Each one believed Robards had actually divorced Rachel. Two years later they discovered that he did not file on charges of desertion after all. No. It was adultery. He claimed Rachel ran off with another man—one Andrew Jackson.

To make it worse, Robards never saw the case to court, so the marriage of Lewis and Rachel Robards had never been dissolved. This meant that Rachel and Andrew had literally, though unwittingly, committed adultery. Both knew immediately that there was no defense against the charge, and each struggled with self-recrimination. Rachel was spiritually devastated that she had left herself prey to the circumstances she now faced. As an attorney himself, Jackson knew he had no excuse for letting this happen, and he could do nothing but move the case through as quietly as possible and vow to protect her honor by whatever means were necessary.

And with the rising public popularity of Andrew Jackson, Rachel's reputation became subject of more and more conversation of lawmakers in the great state of Tennessee. Jackson served as a delegate to the Tennessee constitutional convention and in the United States House of Representatives, but was quick to abandon all dignity and control whenever someone insulted his wife.

In 1806, while serving as a justice of the supreme court of Tennessee, Jackson was driven more by the frontier code of honor than any recent law that prohibited dueling when he killed Charles Dickinson on the banks of the Red River at the southern border of Kentucky. A crack shot himself, the attorney Dickinson fired first and put a bullet in Jackson's chest just one inch from the general's heart, a bullet that his surgeon couldn't remove and he took to the grave with him decades later. Despite his wound, Jackson leveled his pistol and took down Dickinson, later telling his physician, "I'd have hit him [even] if he had shot me through the brain."[2]

Dickinson had insulted Rachel, and, according to historians, when Rachel heard of his death she shed tears for his widow and for the child he would never see. Rachel knew his wife was pregnant.

The guilt she felt over Dickinson's fate must have been overwhelming, but it is possible Rachel might have responded this way no matter the circumstances of his death, because concern for widows and children was elemental to her nature, and her dedication to them throughout her life was absolute. She became "Aunt Rachel" to most of the children in the area because Rachel and Andrew Jackson were unable to have their own. In 1810 Rachel took the baby of a relative who had twins, a boy who was eventually legally adopted and christened Andrew Jackson, Jr. She found solace in children. She also found peace by participating in the rituals of faith—attending church, conducting family prayers, and reading the Bible with her husband.

On their Hermitage estate, located just outside Nashville, in the early 1820s the community built a little brick church and dedicated it to the Presbyterian faith. Jackson himself made the largest contribution to build it, though he didn't join until years after Rachel's death.

Happy with her quiet, peaceful neighborhood where friends accepted her without doubts, Rachel knew obscurity was her only hope to overcome the past. As her husband entered national politics in his battles against John Quincy Adams in 1824, however, this hope faded. She wrote: "The enemys of the Genls have dipt their arrows in wormwood and gall and sped them at me . . . they have Disquieted one that thaey had no rite to do." She prayed for her attackers. "My judg will know how many prayers have I oferd up."[3]

For Rachel Jackson, the worst was yet to come, for she was about to experience one of the most ferocious personal attacks in the history of American presidential politics. It must be noted that political bloodletting happened early and often as the new democracy took shape, and Jackson's supporters were as skillful with the puncture blade as his opponents were. In the 1824 presidential election between Jackson and John Quincy Adams, the results were so close, Congress conducted a runoff. Jackson's political network launched an all-out attack charging bribery and corruption when John Quincy Adams claimed the prize—an attack that raised the stakes on political reputations when the next election came around and left Adams to write: "It seems as if every liar and calumniator in the country were at work day and night, to destroy my character."[4]

During the 1824 election, the Raleigh *Register* also became one of the first newspapers to attack Rachel. The editor wrote: "I make a solemn appeal to the reflecting part of the community, and beg of them to think and ponder well before they place their tickets in the box, how they can justify it to themselves and posterity to place such a woman as Mrs. Jackson! at the head of the female society of the U. States."[5]

When the two adversaries met on the field again in 1828, Jackson won the political battle but lost the war over Rachel's reputation. Attacks on her morals escalated to such a degree that he simply didn't have enough dueling pistols to defend her. Handbills were circulated that said Jackson had "spent the prime of his life in gambling, in cock-fighting, in horse-racing . . . and to cap all tore from a husband the wife of his bosom." A vote for Jackson was a vote for violating the seventh commandment, "You shall not commit adultery." One pamphlet said to be distributed by Adams's men asked the question "Ought a convicted adulteress and her paramour husband to be placed in the highest offices of this free and christian land?"[6]

Remarkably, it is believed Rachel herself may not have known about these written attacks, but Jackson responded with his usual fire. "How hard it is to keep the cowhide from these villains," he wrote. "I have made many sacrifices for my country—but being . . . unable to punish those slanderers of Mrs. J. is too great to be well endured."[7]

After her husband defeated John Quincy Adams in that nasty campaign of 1828 (a campaign, incidentally, in which Jackson's team accused British-born Louisa Adams of queenly airs, snobbery, and lack of total dedication to the American cause), Rachel confessed in one letter: "For Mr. Jackson's sake, I am glad. For my own part I never wished it." With an apparent fondness for Psalm 84 verse 10, she was known for saying to her friends, "I'd rather be a doorkeeper in the house of God, than to dwell in *that palace in Washington,*" substituting the White House for the phrase "the tents of wickedness."[8]

Depression set in for Rachel, but the details of her greatest blow are in conflict. She was in Nashville to be measured for the new clothes she would wear to the inaugural and in her role as the president's wife. Some say she overheard a conversation. Others say she discovered campaign literature. Everyone agrees she came home from that trip a fated woman without hope. Fame was, indeed, her greatest enemy, and it was now fully upon her. Two weeks later she suffered an apparent heart attack, then rallied for a few days before collapsing in her maid's arms and dying by the time her husband was summoned from the next room. She died on December 22, 1828, and her funeral—a ceremony that was spectacular in the crowd it drew and in the simplicity of its message—was held on Christmas Eve. One more blow for the president-elect.

Rev. William Hume began his twenty-minute eulogy with Psalm 112 Verse 6: "The righteous shall be in everlasting remembrance" (KJV), and went on to console the thousands who attended by saying, "While we cordially sympathize with the President of the United States in the irreparable loss he has sustained in the death of his amiable lady, whom he deemed so worthy, as he said, of our tears; we cannot doubt but that she now dwells in the mansions of glory in company with the ransomed of the Lord."[9]

The old general himself made a comment at her grave that his closest companions heard. It was perfectly Andrew Jackson: "In the presence of this dear saint I can and do forgive all my enemies. But those vile wretches who have slandered her must look to God for mercy."[10]

While many speculated that day that Jackson himself would not survive the blow to enter the White House in just three short months, Old Hickory actually claimed two terms in office. In fact, on the night of his second inaugural he sent the others ahead to the celebration while he went to bed and read a chapter from Rachel's Bible, a ritual he began shortly after her death.

Throughout his years as president and until his own death in June 1845, Andrew Jackson carried three symbols that represented his absolute dedication to Rachel—her Bible which he used every night, a miniature of her which he wore every day, and the bullet Charles Dickinson planted just one inch from his heart.

One sad footnote to this story is that John Quincy Adams matched his own father's bitterness when facing political defeat. While Washington,

Jefferson, Monroe, and Madison all attended the inaugurals of their successors, John Quincy Adams took the same path as his father, who refused to attend Thomas Jefferson's inauguration. On the morning of March 3, 1829, John Quincy Adams left Washington before Jackson's bittersweet inaugural ceremony got under way.

It was true that the younger Adams could be cold, austere, stubborn, and harsh. He was, after all, John and Abigail's son and thoroughly defined by Puritan standards. But to suggest that Andrew Jackson was the only one to suffer through the election of 1828 would be terribly shortsighted, for Adams also possessed honesty, courage, and high principles. He was spotless in his private life, got high marks for his record of service to the United States government—which didn't end when he left the office—and he was known for being a powerful standard bearer for future presidents. Yet his own life in the White House was a chronic four-year disappointment, topped off by the death of his son just months before the end of his term. When John Quincy and Louisa Adams left the mansion, they carried out as much personal bitterness as Andrew Jackson carried in.

Attacks on the Presidents' Wives

Nobel Peace Prize recipient Elie Wiesel often observes that evil has outdone itself this century by using technology as its toy as one group persecutes another. Consider the mustard gas of World War I and the concentration camps of World War II. It may seem melodramatic to draw a comparison between persecution and mass murder of millions against the experience of the First Ladies—women who live in what is arguably the most prestigious home in the United States and perhaps the world. But the crude, primitive, and emotional persecution of the First Ladies is as deadly to them as all the sophisticated machinery of mass destruction has been to our world.

Character assassination and outright lies seem to lead the list as weapons of choice, and they strike their victims as efficiently as Andrew Jackson did Charles Dickinson on the banks of the Red River. Lies and slander are as elemental to America's political process as the voting booth and the parade down Main Street.

No one would be surprised, then, to discover that through their journals, their letters, in interviews or their own memoirs, First Ladies consistently identify lies and slander as the worst part of their years in Washington. Let's not overlook, of course, that many First Ladies could dish it out as well. Unable to brush off even a minor provocation, Mary Lincoln quickly transformed political opponents into enemies hailing straight from the pit of hell. According to biographer Jean H. Baker: "Not many nineteenth-century women employed the language of vilification that she adopted from politics. To some Springfield neighbors, Mary Lincoln was so incurably hostile as to do permanent damage to any friendship."[11]

Overall, though, First Ladies were more likely to be victims than attackers. Years after she left the White House, someone asked Frances Cleveland if she'd like to be First Lady again. This was a fair question, considering her husband was both the twenty-second and the twenty-fourth president. Frances, however, replied abruptly, "What! There where my husband was accustomed to drag me about the house by the hair and where my children were blind, deaf, and deformed? Never!"[12] In her memoirs, *My Turn,* Nancy Reagan summed up the experience of many First Ladies regarding their honeymoons with the fourth estate and the public. "Virtually everything I did during that first year was misunderstood and ridiculed. I sometimes had the feeling that if it were raining outside, it was probably my fault."[13]

Republican campaign buttons for the 1940 presidential election read WE DON'T WANT ELEANOR EITHER! She described that campaign as "bad in personal bitterness as any I have ever been in."[14] Lou Hoover and Nancy Reagan were both quoted saying, "I wouldn't like me either if I believed what was said about me." Margaret Taylor, wife of twelfth president, Zachary Taylor, avoided public appearances completely during her time at the White House. She so strongly opposed his bid for the office that—like Jane Pierce—she prayed her husband would lose the election. Her daughter Betty served as hostess to the president, and the press knew nothing about Margaret. Rumors circulated that she was a pipe-smoking poor white, when in reality Margaret was the daughter of Maryland aristocrats.

First Ladies are criticized for personal appearance: Eleanor Roosevelt wore too many hats. Rosalynn Carter once forgot to wear a hat. Hillary Clinton has too many hairstyles. Lucy Hayes had only one hairstyle. (It was a part down the middle, finger puffs on the sides, swept up and wrapped in the back. My guess is Rutherford went to his grave as the only one who knew just how long those locks really were.) Nancy Reagan had too lavish a taste for clothes and jewels.

They are criticized for their attitudes: Lou Hoover, whose personal contributions to charity as First Lady were so large she deliberately hid some of the information from her husband, was considered out of touch with real people struggling through the Depression. On the other hand, Eleanor Roosevelt, whose husband defeated Herbert Hoover in 1932, was accused of constantly meddling in governmental programs designed to assist the nation's poor. Abigail Adams, Nellie Taft, Nancy Reagan, Edith Wilson, and Hillary Clinton all were accused of wanting their husband's jobs.

They are criticized on the subject of alcohol: While Sarah Polk, Lucy Hayes, and Rosalynn Carter took hits because they didn't serve liquor in the White House, Florence Harding not only served liquor during Prohibition, she constantly feared someone would bring up her first marriage—to an alcoholic named Henry de Wolfe. They had one son, and she divorced de Wolfe after he abandoned her. He eventually died, and Florence began to lie about her past, saying she was a widow.[15] Bess Truman worried that she would face inquiry over her father's death. He was an alcoholic who committed suicide.[16] The cruelest remarks regarding alcohol, however, were flung at Mamie Eisenhower, who suffered Ménière's disease, which kept her off balance and sometimes made her appear inebriated. In 1959, one columnist for the *National Enquirer* said that at a cocktail party Mamie drank so much in one evening, the hostess tried to stop her and that Ike tried to get her out as quietly as possible.

Nicknames are just as telling, starting with Hillary "Ramrod" Clinton. Mary Lincoln was "Hellcat." Harry Truman called his wife "the Boss," but others referred to her as "Payroll Bess" because she held a salaried position on his staff when he served as a United States senator. Mrs. Hayes was "Lemonade Lucy," though she was hardly a fanatic regarding temperance. Abigail Adams was "Mrs. President," in tribute to her outspokenness, and some First Ladies were simply called "the Bitch." By her tenure, will, and outspoken nature, however, Eleanor Roosevelt was the queen of titles: "Eleanor the Great," "La Boca Grande," "The Gab," and even "Stalin in Petticoats."

Nancy Reagan was called "the Iron Orange," "the Evita of Santa Barbara," and "Little Gun," a pun referring to her ability to fire staff without hesitation and the little gun she once said she kept at her bedside. In 1981, when the First Lady represented the United States at the wedding of Prince Charles and Lady Diana in London, she came home to the nickname "Queen Nancy" because she hung out with royals with such apparent ease and comfort. "Now that's silly," Nancy joked about the title. "Everyone knows that a crown would mess my hair."[17] The image of Queen Nancy, though, was escalated when she acquired new china for the White House—china paid for by a private donor but also china shown to the press on the very day the Reagan administration proposed a $41 billion cut in welfare programs and announced that catsup was a vegetable for the subsidized school lunches of underprivileged children.

Attacks on presidents and First Ladies in the name of religion and morals have been as much a part of our history as the presidency itself:

Dolley Madison

Rumors floated through Washington that perhaps Dolley Madison was having an affair with Thomas Jefferson while he served as president (from 1801 to 1809). She served as hostess in the White House during his term because Jefferson was a widower and her husband James served as Jefferson's secretary of state. When Dolley became First Lady after her husband's election in 1808, some said the Madisons were childless because James was impotent and she oversexed. Others said Dolley was happy only when surrounded by men. At the suggestion that he had had an affair with Madison's wife, Jefferson shrugged at the rumors, saying, "[I] thought my age and ordinary demeanor would have prevented any suggestions in that form. . . ."[18]

Dolley's personal popularity seemed only slightly dented by the attacks though. When Charles Pinckney lost the presidency to Madison, he claimed he "was beaten by Mr. and Mrs. Madison. I might have had a better chance had I faced Mr. Madison alone."[19]

Edith Wilson

In 1915 the joke at Washington dinner parties went like this:

"What did Edith Galt do when President Wilson asked her to marry him?"

"She fell out of bed."

Wilson's second wife came under broiling criticism because she claimed his heart just eight months after Ellen's death. The cruelest gossip claimed that the two had been involved while Ellen was alive, and that Ellen had been poisoned or pushed down a flight of stairs. Citizens, especially women, were angry that Wilson fell for another woman even before the tombstone was placed at Ellen's grave.

In her memoirs, Edith Wilson wrote that when the president expressed his love for her in May 1915, she responded with surprise. "Oh, you can't love me for you don't really know me," she said. "And it is less than a year since your wife died."

Wilson said to her, "Yes, I know you feel that, but, little girl, in this place time is not measured by weeks, or months, or years, but by deep human experiences; and since her death I have lived a lifetime of loneliness and heartache."[20]

Pat Nixon

From the time her husband entered his first political campaign, Patricia Nixon faced misunderstandings about her maiden name, Ryan, and stories circulated regularly that she was a fallen-away Catholic. According to Julie Nixon Eisenhower, when her father ran for the United States Senate in 1950, a man walked into the Long Beach office and asked a staffer, "Does the Ryan name mean what I think it does?"

"Mean what?" she asked.

"Mean Pat Nixon's a Catholic," he said. "I'd never vote for a man if he were married to a Catholic."

"Pat's not a Catholic," said the staffer. "But I don't think Mr. Nixon would want your vote."[21]

Jackie Kennedy

In the summer of 1962 Jackie Kennedy took a private vacation to Ravello, Italy, with her daughter, Caroline, a trip that included shopping, strolls down café-filled streets, a ceremony in which she was made an honorary citizen of Ravello—and at least fifty photographers following her everywhere. When she and Caroline went to the beach, photographs were zapped around the globe showing America's First Lady in a bathing suit.

By the time her plane landed on American soil, Jackie Kennedy was greeted by more than one hundred protesters who claimed to be part of an organization called Concerned Citizens of America. They picketed the airport with signs that said YOU HAVE INDULGED IN AN EXCESS OF HEDONISM. WOULD YOU NOT BETTER HAVE SERVED THE NATION BY REMAINING HERE AT HOME BY HIS SIDE? and DOES THIS SET A PROPER EXAMPLE FOR THE YOUNG WOMEN OF AMERICA?[22]

Betty Ford

In August 1975, CBS aired a *60 Minutes* episode that included some remarkable admissions by First Lady Betty Ford. She commented, as she had in the past, that legalized abortion was "a great, great decision" that took the procedure out of the alleys and into hospitals and clinics, where it belongs. She spoke about her decision to see a psychiatrist in past years, and she also stood by earlier comments that she refused to freak out over the news that a young person actually tried marijuana.

But the bombshell hit America's conservative terra firma when Morley Safer asked, "What if Susan Ford came to you and said, 'Mother, I'm having an affair'?"

She hesitated and then calmly replied, "Well, I wouldn't be surprised. I think she's a perfectly normal human being, like all young girls. If she wanted to continue it, I would certainly counsel and advise her on the subject, and I'd want to know pretty much about the young man."

William Loeb, editor of the Manchester *Union-Leader*, wrote, "The immorality of Mrs. Ford's remarks is almost exceeded by their stupidity . . . a disgusting spectacle. Coming from the First Lady in the White House, it disgraces the nation itself. . . . As president of the United States, he should be the moral leader of the nation. He is not in a position of any ordinary husband making the best of his wife's foolish and stupid remarks. . . . He should repudiate what Mrs. Ford said."

Betty later said, "What I'd been trying to say was that while I couldn't condone an affair I wouldn't kick my daughter out of the house for having one. . . . I consider myself a responsible parent . . . in a home that believes in and practices the enduring values of morality and personal integrity . . . these are not easy times to be a parent. Our convictions are continually being questioned and tested by fads and fancies of the moment. I want my children to know that their concerns . . . whatever they may be, can be discussed. . . . I do not believe in premarital relations, but I realize that many in today's generation do not share my views. . . ."[23]

Frances Cleveland

When Frances Cleveland was First Lady, rumors persisted during her husband's bid for reelection in 1888 that Grover physically abused her. Pamphlets circulated at the Democratic Convention made this claim. So did newspapers and even a few pastors from the pulpit. Finally, Frances took the remarkable step of defending her marriage publicly.

She responded to a note from one citizen—who addressed the charges against Grover—by submitting an open letter to the press that was published by the New York *Evening Post* on June 6, 1888. Other papers reprinted the piece. In her letter she said, "I can only say in answer to your letter that every statement in the interview which you send me is basely false, and I pity the man who has been made the tool to give circulation to such wicked and heartless lies. I can wish the women of our country no better blessing than that their homes and their lives may be as happy, and that their husbands may be as kind and attentive, as considerate and affectionate, as mine."[24]

Eleanor Roosevelt

As First Lady, Eleanor Roosevelt consistently opposed federal aid to parochial schools, arguing that it violated the church-state separation clauses of the United States Constitution. As a former First Lady, she became involved in several issues in which she directly opposed the hierarchy of the Roman Catholic Church. "The leaders of the Catholic church responsible for its political interests had long been unhappy about Mrs. Roosevelt," wrote biographer Joseph P. Lash. "Her friendliness toward Loyalist Spain in the thirties, her support, even though discreet, of birth control, her sponsorship of the American Youth Congress and other organizations in which the Communists had been heavily represented had vexed the clergy to the point of public expression of its displeasure even while she was First Lady."[25]

In her *My Day* column on June 23, 1949, she addressed the school aid issue again by explaining that the nation provided public schools because they strengthen democracy. Others certainly have the right to establish their own schools, she said, but should not receive public assistance because they were not entitled to it. She also explained that the separation of church and state was a fundamental part of the United States Constitution and that she was not prejudiced because she believed people had the right to worship God any way they saw fit.

The nation was stunned when New York's Francis Joseph Cardinal Spellman fired back the following month with an open letter to Eleanor Roosevelt, charging her with misinterpreting the church's position on federal aid and accusing her of conducting an anti-Catholic campaign. Then he ended with words that created an international controversy:

> Now my case is closed. This letter will be released to the public tomorrow after it has been delivered to you by special delivery today. And even though you may use your columns to attack me and accuse me of starting a controversy, *I shall not again publicly acknowledge you.* For, whatever you may say in the future, your record of anti-Catholicism stands for all to see—a record which you yourself wrote in the pages

> of history which cannot be recalled—documents of discrimination *unworthy of an American mother!*[26]

Eleanor received four thousand letters, and more than ninety percent were supporting her position. The Raleigh *News and Observer* wrote: "Not in a long time has America been presented with a spectacle of a man behaving with less tolerance, less Christian humility, and more readiness to damn and malign those who disagree with him than that shown by Cardinal Spellman of New York."[27]

In her letter of response to the cardinal, she spelled out her views on federal aid, rejected charges of being anti-Catholic by explaining she has backed many Catholic candidates, and addressed other points before ending her correspondence with a piercing remark: "I assure you that I had no sense of being 'an unworthy American mother,' " she said. "The final judgment, my dear Cardinal Spellman, of the worthiness of all human beings is in the hands of God."[28]

Likely ordered to make a public gesture of reconciliation, the cardinal issued a new statement—preapproved by Eleanor—which said in part: "We are not asking for general public support of religious schools. . . . Under the Constitution, we do not ask, nor can we expect, public funds to pay for the construction or repair of parochial school buildings, or for the support of teachers, or for other maintenance costs." He went on to express his regret over "the great confusion and regrettable misunderstandings" that had arisen. He also reaffirmed "the American right of free speech which not only permits but encourages differences of opinion."[29]

In her *My Day* column published August 29, 1949, she wrote: "The other afternoon as I was signing mail, with side glances out of my window, and I am afraid my thoughts centered on how quickly I could get out for a swim, Miss Thompson came to my desk, looking somewhat breathless and said: 'Mrs. Roosevelt, Cardinal Spellman is on the porch and he wants to see you!'

"The Cardinal had dropped in on his way to dedicate a chapel in Peekskill. We had a pleasant chat and I hope the country proved as much a tonic for him as it always does for me."

Pat Nixon

Pat Nixon probably had the unfortunate distinction of suffering more persecution in the form of physical abuse than any other First Lady in our history. Fortunately, the delicate-looking blonde had iron in her spine and a remarkable amount of compassion in her heart even in moments that would—and did—scare her companions so badly, they became hysterical.

When her husband served as vice president under Dwight Eisenhower, she went with him on a goodwill trip to Venezuela that turned out to be a nightmare for the Secret Service and the American diplomatic corps—and it included a plot to assassinate the vice president. After the Nixons' plane landed in Caracas, they were greeted by a small welcoming committee and an overwhelming crowd of angry demonstrators. Surrounded by bodyguards who simply wanted to keep them moving, the Nixons were forced to stand still at the entrance of the airport terminal in honor of their host country when the Venezuelan national anthem was played. A mob standing over them on an observation deck began to shower them with garbage and spit.

Julie Nixon Eisenhower described the scene: "At first the spit looked like giant snowflakes, but it turned to foul, dark blotches when it hit my mother's red suit and the clothes of those standing with her." The Secret Service moved them through the mob and got them into the motorcade, Vice President Nixon and the Venezuelan foreign minister in one car, Mrs. Nixon and the minister's wife in the next car. The American press assigned to cover the event made a point of describing Pat's self-control throughout the ordeal." Reporters saw Pat Nixon ignore the final onslaught and stop to hug a child who had given her flowers. They also saw her lean across a barricade to pat the shoulder of a young girl who had just cursed and spat at her. The girl turned away in shame."[30]

After leaving the airport, the motorcade headed into the city, where the most terrifying part of the trip occurred. Forced to stop twice, the cars were pelted by demonstrators with rocks the first time, by a mob of more than five hundred the second time—some with pipes and baseball bats. (The Nixons were virtually unprotected by the Venezuelan authorities, and President Eisenhower commended the twelve Secret Service agents for heroism.)

They were trying to overturn the vice president's car and set fire to it, and at this point the minister's wife lost control and began screaming while Pat Nixon tried to console her. Both women were in the second vehicle of the motorcade.

The madness ended when the vice president's car was able to cross the dividing line on the highway and speed off—to the American embassy instead of the planned events. They spent the night under heavy guard provided by the Venezuelan government, and the next day when they returned to the airport the streets were vacant—having been cleared by tear gas and now guarded by police officers wearing gas masks. As she climbed aboard the jet to return to United States soil, Pat Nixon had just completed the most ill-fated goodwill tour in American history.

Mary Lincoln

Through the mid-1800s there was an unspoken but accepted rule that presidents' wives were not considered appropriate news copy, Rachel Jackson's misfortune notwithstanding. By the election of 1860, however, and with an intense spotlight on the Civil War, the press demonstrated an overwhelming reversal. The wife of President-elect Abraham Lincoln was thrown into the headlines with both enthusiasm and malice, depending on the editor's politics and Mary's latest antics.

A trinity of the darkest human afflictions swirled around the First Lady in the winter of 1862: Her own mental instability, the death of a second son, and the press's willingness to vilify her left Mary fighting overwhelming battles while her husband—challenged by his own grief over Willie's death—searched desperately for a commanding general who could claim victory against the Confederates.

When eleven-year-old Willie Lincoln died in February, Mary entered what one historian called "first degree mourning," wearing black for an entire year and writing to a friend back in Springfield: "Our home is very beautiful. The grounds are very enchanting, the world still smiles and pays homage and we are left desolate—the world has lost its charm."[31]

Hostile observers, however, said Mary Lincoln was merely paying the price for her poor behavior as First Lady, that this was surely God's scourge on an evil woman. Others noted that at least she got to hold her boy while he died, unlike most of the American mothers who had lost a son that year. The cruelest charges, though, suggested that Mary actually beat her own children, a statement historians typically dismiss as completely unfounded, but one suggesting she may actually have contributed to his death.

When one by one, three of her half brothers died in service to the Confederate Army, some editors and Union Army leaders charged she wasn't fully committed to the North. Mary was a native of Kentucky, and of Mary and her thirteen full and half brothers and sisters, eight supported the Confederates, six the Union. Meanwhile, Emilie Todd Helm, one of those Southern half sisters, blamed the Lincolns directly for the deaths of her own husband and brother.

Persecution surrounded her throughout her time in the White House, and circumstances left her an easy target—just as Abraham Lincoln seemed an easy target at Ford's Theatre on April 14, 1865. On that evening John Wilkes Booth acted on his own beliefs, and persecution extracted its greatest price from the already fragile world of Mary Lincoln.

A healthy dose of political cynicism is one thing, but the examples covered in this chapter clearly are something else. It seems such a basic point about human nature, but we are meant to think twice before we insult, and think three times before we label others with subhuman terms. Persecution against an individual begins with the belief that she is something *less* than or *different* from human. It has been a deadly force in the world, in our country, in your state and community. It also has been a deadly force in the lives of our First Ladies.

Echoes of This Beatitude in the Bible

Psalm 119:86: "All your commands are trustworthy; help me, for men persecute me without cause."

Matthew 5:44: "But I tell you: Love your enemies and pray for those who persecute you. . . ."

John 15:20–21: "Remember the words I spoke to you: 'No servant is greater than his master. If they persecuted me, they will persecute you also. If they obeyed my teaching, they will obey yours also. They will treat you this way because of my name for they do not know the One who sent me."

Romans 12:14: "Bless those who persecute you; bless and do not curse."

Lamentations 5:5: "Those who pursue us are at our heels; we are weary, and find no rest."

Ecclesiastes 9:1: "So I reflected on all this and concluded that the righteous and the wise and what they do are in God's hands, but no man knows whether love or hate awaits him."

Romans 8:35: "Who shall separate us from the love of Christ? Shall trouble or hardship or persecution or famine or nakedness or danger or sword?"

II Timothy 3:12: "In fact, everyone who wants to live a godly life in Christ Jesus will be persecuted. . . ."

FIRST LADY QUOTABLES

"You seek guidance from God to do what's right and best. I think you have to do that constantly because criticisms are constant. It doesn't matter what you do, you are going to be criticized. In the face of criticism you have to be in prayer and just trust God to guide you to do what is best and right for the country. I think if you are deeply rooted in your faith before you get there, it is a lot easier. I was always so thankful for growing up in the church."

—ROSALYNN CARTER

"There are always some mischief-makers in Washington who are trying to make trouble for reasons known only to themselves. Patty Presock (George's wonderful assistant) told me that two masked/voice-altered people appeared on Pat Robertson's program who claimed to be staff members fearful of reprisals who said that George was being taken over by liberals."

—BARBARA BUSH

Photon on page 204:

Devastated when her husband's opponents used her background as a divorcée to paint her as an adulteress before the whole nation, Rachel Jackson collapsed and died after her husband Andrew was elected, but before he took office.

Photo courtesy of the White House Historical Association

Notes

Introduction

1. Charles Francis Adams, *Familiar Letters of John Adams and His Wife Abigail During the Revolution,* 42–43.
2. Theodore Roosevelt, *The Autobiography of Theodore Roosevelt,* 188.
3. Eleanor Roosevelt, *Eleanor Roosevelt's My Day: Vol. III: Her Acclaimed Columns 1953–1962,* ed. by David Emblidge. Eleanor Roosevelt's "My Day" column is collected in three volumes, of which this is the last. See bibliography. Hereafter, references from these three sources will appear in the text as *My Day,* followed by the date.

Chapter One

1. Hillary Clinton to the United Methodist General Conference, Denver, April 24, 1996.
2. Mary Ormsbee Whitton, *First First Ladies 1789–1865: A Study of the Wives of the Early Presidents,* 260.
3. Ibid., 261.
4. Carl Sferrazza Anthony, *First Ladies Vol. I: The Saga of the Presidents' Wives and Their Power 1789–1961,* 157–58.
5. Mary Ormsbee Whitton, *First First Ladies,* 262.
6. Elswyth Thane, *Washington's Lady: The Life of Martha Washington,* 287.
7. W. H. Crook, *Memories of the White House: Personal Reflections of Colonel W. H. Crook,* 66–68.
8. Richard M. Nixon. *The Memoirs of Richard Nixon,* 1086.
9. Nancy Reagan with William Novak, *My Turn,* 5.
10. Paul C. Nagel, *The Adams Women: Abigail and Louisa Adams, Their Sisters and Daughters,* 215.
11. Joseph P. Lash, *Eleanor and Franklin,* 378.
12. Eleanor Roosevelt, *This Is My Story,* 11, 17.

13. Ibid., 18, 162. Joseph P. Lash, *Love, Eleanor: Eleanor Roosevelt and Her Friends,* 309.
14. Ibid., 73.
15. Richard Harrity and Ralph G. Martin, *Eleanor Roosevelt: Her Life in Pictures,* 89. Joseph P. Lash, *Love, Eleanor,* 132.
16. Ibid., 240, 241.
17. Joseph P. Lash, *Eleanor: The Years Alone,* 332.
18. Betty Ford with Chris Chase, *The Times of My Life,* 316–17.
19. Ibid., 305.
20. Ibid., 308, 310–11.
21. Carl Sferrazza Anthony, *First Ladies Vol. I,* 283.
22. Charles Willis Thompson, *Presidents I Have Known and Two Near Presidents,* 17.
23. Jean H. Baker, *Mary Todd Lincoln: A Biography,* 56, 194.
24. W. H. Crook, *Memories,* 52–53.
25. Carl Sferrazza Anthony, *First Ladies Vol. I,* 105.
26. Julia Dent Grant, *The Personal Memoirs of Julia Dent Grant,* 196.
27. Ibid., 197.
28. Dolley Madison, *Memoirs and Letters of Dolley Madison,* 209–10.

Chapter Two

1. Richard M. Nixon, *Memoirs,* 254–55.
2. Richard Norton Smith, *An Uncommon Man: The Triumph of Herbert Hoover,* 426.
3. Lady Bird Johnson, *A White House Diary,* 6.
4. Ibid., 10.
5. Ibid., 10.
6. Ibid., 11.
7. Margaret Leech and Harry J. Brown, *The Garfield Orbit,* 242.
8. Paul F. Boller, Jr., *Presidential Wives: An Anecdotal History,* 155.
9. Margaret Leech, *The Garfield Orbit,* 243.
10. Ibid., 242, 244–45.
11. Allan Peskin, *Garfield: A Biography,* 598.
12. Carl Sferrazza Anthony, *First Ladies Vol. I,* 244.
13. Allan Peskin, *Garfield,* 593.
14. Paul F. Boller, Jr., *Presidential Wives,* 160–61.
15. James A. Green, *William Henry Harrison: His Life and Times,* 403.
16. Mary Ormsbee Whitton, *First First Ladies,* 170.
17. Ibid., 227.
18. Ibid., 183.
19. Ibid., 183.
20. Carl Sferrazza Anthony, *First Ladies Vol. I,* 123.

21. Oliver P. Chitwood, *John Tyler: Champion of the Old South,* 396.
22. Harry J. Sievers, *Benjamin Harrison: Hoosier President,* 242, 243.
23. Ibid., 243.
24. Mary Ormsbee Whitton, *First First Ladies,* 114.
25. Julia Dent Grant, *Memoirs,* 331.
26. Edith Bolling Wilson, *My Memoir,* 359–60.
27. Cheryl Heckler-Feltz, "Strong First Lady: Lucy Hayes." *Ohio Magazine,* October 1996.
28. Joseph P. Lash, *Eleanor: The Years Alone,* 331.
29. Mary Ormsbee Whitton, *First First Ladies,* 9.
30. Ishbel Ross, *Grace Coolidge and Her Era,* 123.
31. Ibid., 161.
32. Claude M. Fuess, *Calvin Coolidge: The Man from Vermont,* 351–52.
33. Jean H. Baker, *Mary Todd Lincoln,* 127.
34. Julia Dent Grant, *Memoirs,* 13.

Chapter Three

1. Emily Apt Geer, *First Lady: The Life of Lucy Webb Hayes,* 73.
2. Edith Mayo, director of the political science division and curator of the First Ladies Exhibit at the American Museum of History, interview with the author, Washington, D.C., May 16, 1995.
3. Emily Apt Geer, *First Lady,* 251.
4. Ibid., 157.
5. Paul F. Boller, Jr., *Presidential Wives,* 7.
6. Lynne Withey, *Dearest Friend: A Life of Abigail Adams,* 310.
7. Lady Bird Johnson, *A White House Diary,* 588–89.
8. Doris Kearns, *Lyndon Johnson and the American Dream,* 96.
9. Ibid.
10. Lady Bird Johnson, *A White House Diary,* 210.
11. Sylvia Jukes Morris, *Edith Kermit Roosevelt: Portrait of a First Lady,* 270, 221.
12. Ibid., 278.
13. Theodore Roosevelt, *Autobiography,* 183.
14. Ibid., 185.
15. Irwin H. (Ike) Hoover, *Forty-two Years in the White House,* 28.
16. Sylvia Jukes Morris, *Edith Kermit Roosevelt,* 341.
17. Ibid., 387. Charles Willis Thompson, *Presidents I Have Known and Two Near Presidents,* 105–55. Sylvia Jukes Morris, *Edith Kermit Roosevelt,* 413, 516.

Chapter Four

1. Donnie Radcliffe, *Hillary Rodham Clinton: A First Lady for Our Time,* 44.
2. Hillary Rodham Clinton to the United Methodist General Conference.
3. Ibid.
4. Ibid.
5. Hillary Rodham Clinton, *It Takes a Village: And Other Lessons Children Teach Us,* 178.
6. Hillary Rodham Clinton to the United Methodist General Conference.
7. Lynne Withey, *Dearest Friend,* 181–82.
8. Eleanor Roosevelt, *This Is My Story.* 108.
9. Carl Sferrazza Anthony, *First Ladies Vol. I,* 260.
10. Ishbel Ross, *Grace Coolidge,* 312.
11. Ibid., 342.

Chapter Five

1. August Heckscher, *Woodrow Wilson: A Biography,* 63.
2. Paul F. Boller, *Presidential Wives,* 223.
3. August Heckscher, Jr., *Woodrow Wilson,* 79, 224.
4. Betty Ford, *The Times of My Life,* 93.
5. Rosalynn Carter, *First Lady from Plains,* 280.
6. Mary Ormsbee Whitton, *First First Ladies,* 79.
7. Paul F. Boller, Jr., *Presidential Wives,* 51.
8. W. H. Crook, *Memories,* 195–96.
9. Mary Ormsbee Whitton, *First First Ladies,* 245.
10. Lady Bird Johnson, *A White House Diary,* 735–37.

Chapter Six

1. Rosalynn Carter, *First Lady from Plains,* 9.
2. Interview with the author, Atlanta, Georgia, February 12, 1995. Rosalynn Carter, *First Lady from Plains,* 88.
3. Ibid., 89–90.
4. Mary Ormsbee Whitton, *First First Ladies,* 147.
5. Ibid., 204.
6. Ibid., 208.
7. Margaret C. Conkling, *Memoirs of the Mother and Wife of Washington,* 514n.
8. Betty Ford, *The Times of My Life,* 290.
9. Mary Ormsbee Whitton, *First First Ladies,* 155.
10. James A. Green, *William Henry Harrison: His Life and Times,* 209.
11. Ibid., 444.

12. Ibid., 444–45.
13. Ibid., 442.

Chapter Seven

1. Joseph P. Lash, *Eleanor: The Years Alone,* 50.
2. *My Day,* Feb. 8, 1946.
3. Joseph P. Lash, *Eleanor: The Years Alone,* 53–54.
4. Ibid., 80.
5. Ibid., 81.
6. Joseph P. Lash, *Love, Eleanor,* 300.
7. Ibid., 364.
8. Carl Sferrazza Anthony, *First Ladies Vol. I,* 505.
9. Elswyth Thane, *Washington's Lady,* 80.
10. Nathanial Hervey, *The Memory of Washington,* 85–86.
11. Benson J. Lossing, *Mary and Martha: The Mother and Wife of George Washington,* 168.
12. Paul F. Boller, Jr., *Presidential Wives,* 11.
13. Ibid., 47.
14. Rosalynn Carter, *First Lady from Plains,* 253.
15. Sylvia Jukes Morris, *Edith Kermit Roosevelt,* 299–300.
16. Julia Dent Grant, *Memoirs,* 140.
17. Paul F. Boller, Jr., *Presidential Wives,* 29–30.
18. George H. Nash, *The Life of Herbert Hoover: The Engineer, 1874–1914,* 122.

Chapter Eight

1. Marquis James, *The Life of Andrew Jackson,* 67.
2. Ibid., 118.
3. Ibid., 473.
4. Mary Ormsbee Whitton, *First First Ladies,* 127.
5. Marquis James, *The Life of Andrew Jackson,* 407.
6. Ibid., 465.
7. Ibid., 466.
8. Ibid., 474.
9. Ibid., 481.
10. Ibid., 482.
11. Jean H. Baker, *Mary Todd Lincoln,* 150–51.
12. Carl Sferrazza Anthony, *First Ladies Vol. I,* 300.
13. Nancy Reagan, *My Turn,* 23.
14. Carl Sferrazza Anthony, *First Ladies Vol. I,* 488.
15. Francis Russell, *The Shadow of Blooming Grove: Warren Harding in His Times,* 84.

16. Margaret Truman, *Bess W. Truman,* 20.
17. Paul F. Boller, Jr., *Presidential Wives,* 459–60.
18. Carl Sferrazza Anthony, *First Ladies Vol. I,* 80.
19. Paul F. Boller, Jr., *Presidential Wives,* 38.
20. Edith Bolling Wilson, *My Memoir,* 62.
21. Julie Nixon Eisenhower, *Pat Nixon,* 109.
22. Carl Sferrazza Anthony, *First Ladies Vol. II,* 76.
23. Betty Ford, *The Times of My Life,* 226. Carl Sferrazza Anthony, *First Ladies Vol. II,* 251.
24. Carl Sferrazza Anthony, *First Ladies Vol. I,* 266.
25. Joseph P. Lash, *Eleanor: The Years Alone,* 156.
26. Ibid., 158.
27. Ibid., 160.
28. Ibid., 159.
29. Ibid., 164.
30. Julie Nixon Eisenhower, *Pat Nixon,* 174.
31. Jean H. Baker, *Mary Todd Lincoln,* 215.

Bibliography

Adams, John, and Abigail Adams. *Familiar Letters of John Adams and His Wife Abigail During the Revolution,* ed. by Charles Francis Adams, NP. 1875.

Akers, Charles W. *Abigail Adams: An American Woman.* Little, Brown. 1980.

Anthony, Carl Sferrazza. *First Ladies Vol. I: The Saga of the Presidents' Wives and Their Power 1789–1961.* Morrow. 1990.

———. *First Ladies Vol. II: The Saga of the Presidents' Wives and Their Power 1789–1961.* Morrow. 1991.

Baker, Jean H. *Mary Todd Lincoln: A Biography.* W. W. Norton. 1987.

Barnard, Harry. *Rutherford B. Hayes and His America.* Bobbs-Merrill. 1954.

Bell, Jack. *The Johnson Treatment: How Lyndon B. Johnson Took Over the Presidency and Made It His Own.* Harper & Row. 1965.

Birmingham, Stephen. *Jacqueline Bouvier Kennedy Onassis.* Grosset & Dunlap. 1982.

Boller, Paul F. Jr. *Presidential Wives: An Anecdotal History.* Oxford. 1988.

Bush, Barbara. *A Memoir.* St. Martin's Paperbacks. 1994.

Caroli, Betty Boyd. *First Ladies.* Doubleday. 1989.

Carter, Jimmy. *Keeping Faith: Memoirs of a President.* Bantam. 1982.

Carter, Rosalynn. *First Lady from Plains.* Ballantine. 1984.

———with Susan K. Golant. *Helping Yourself Help Others: A Book for Caregivers.* Times Books. 1994.

Chitwood, Oliver P. *John Tyler: Champion of the Old South.* NP. 1939.

Clinton, Hillary Rodham. *It Takes a Village: And Other Lessons Children Teach Us.* Simon and Schuster. 1996.

Conkling, Margaret C. *Memoirs of the Mother and Wife of Washington.* NP. 1850.

Cook, Blanche Wiesen. *Eleanor Roosevelt Vol. I 1884–1933.* Viking. 1992.

Crompton, Samuel. *The Presidents of the United States.* Smithmark. 1992.

Crook, W. H. *Memories of the White House: Personal Reflections of Colonel W. H. Crook.* Little, Brown. 1911.

Davis, Burke. *Old Hickory: The Life of Andrew Jackson.* Dial. 1977.

Eisenhower, Dwight D. *At Ease: Stories I Tell to Friends.* Doubleday. 1967.

Eisenhower, Julie Nixon. *Pat Nixon: The Untold Story.* Simon & Schuster. 1986.

Fields, Joseph E. *Worthy Partner: The Papers of Martha Washington.* Greenwood. 1994.

Ford, Betty, with Chris Chase. *The Times of My Life.* Ballantine. 1979.

Freedman, Russell. *Eleanor Roosevelt: A Life of Discovery.* Scholastic. 1993.

Fuess, Claude M. *Calvin Coolidge: The Man from Vermont.* NP. 1939.

Geer, Emily Apt. *First Lady: The Life of Lucy Webb Hayes.* Kent State University Press and The Rutherford B. Hayes Presidential Center. 1984.

Gelles, Edith B. *Portia: The World of Abigail Adams.* Indiana University Press. 1992.

Gordon, Lydia L. *From Lady Washington to Mrs. Cleveland.* Books for Libraries Press. 1972.

Grant, Julia Dent. *The Personal Memoirs of Julia Dent Grant,* ed. by John Y. Simon. Putnam. 1975.

Green, James A. *William Henry Harrison: His Life and Times.* Garrett and Massie. 1941.

Harrity, Richard, and Ralph G. Martin. *Eleanor Roosevelt: Her Life in Pictures.* NP. ND.

Heckler-Feltz, Cheryl. "A Strong Lady in the White House: Lucy Hayes." *Ohio Magazine* (October 1996): 18–21, 58.

Heckscher, August. *Woodrow Wilson: A Biography.* Charles Scribner's Sons. 1991.

Hervey, Nathanial. *The Memory of Washington.* NP. ND.

Hoover, Irwin H. (Ike). *Forty-two Years in the White House.* Houghton Mifflin. 1934.

James, Marquis. *The Life of Andrew Jackson.* Bobbs-Merrill. 1938.

Johnson, Lady Bird. *A White House Diary.* Holt, Rinehart and Winston. 1970.

Kearns, Doris. *Lyndon Johnson and the American Dream.* Harper & Row. 1976.

Ketcham, Ralph. *James Madison: A Biography.* Macmillan. 1971.

Lash, Joseph P. *Eleanor and Franklin.* W. W. Norton. 1971.

———. *Eleanor: The Years Alone.* W. W. Norton. 1972.

———. *Love, Eleanor: Eleanor Roosevelt and Her Friends.* Doubleday. 1982.

Leamer, Laurence. *The Kennedy Women: The Saga of an American Family.* Villard. 1994.

Leech, Margaret. *In the Days of McKinley.* Harper. 1959.

——— and Harry J. Brown. *The Garfield Orbit.* Harper & Row. 1978.

Lossing, Benson J. *Mary and Martha: The Mother and Wife of George Washington.* NP. ND.

Lyons, Eugene. *Herbert Hoover: A Biography.* Doubleday. 1964.

Madison, Dolley. *Memoirs and Letters of Dolley Madison.* NP. 1886.

Means, Marianne. *The Women in the White House: The Lives, Times and Influence of Twelve Notable First Ladies.* Random House. 1963.

Miller, Nathan. *Theodore Roosevelt: A Life.* Morrow. 1992.

Morgan, H. Wayne. *William McKinley and His America.* Syracuse University Press. 1963.

Morris, Sylvia Jukes. *Edith Kermit Roosevelt: Portrait of a First Lady.* Coward, McCann & Geoghegan. 1980.

Nagel, Paul C. *The Adams Women: Abigail and Louisa Adams, Their Sisters and Daughters.* Oxford University Press. 1987.

Nash, George H. *The Life of Herbert Hoover: The Engineer, 1874–1914.* W. W. Norton. 1983.

Nixon, Richard M. *The Memoirs of Richard Nixon.* Grosset & Dunlap. 1978.

Pendel, Thomas F. *Thirty-six Years in the White House.* Neal. 1902.

Peskin, Allan. *Garfield: A Biography.* Kent State University Press. 1978.

Pringle, Henry F. *The Life and Times of William Howard Taft. Vols. I and II.* Archon. 1964.

Radcliffe, Donnie. *Hillary Rodham Clinton: A First Lady for Our Time.* Warner Books. 1993.

Randall, Ruth Painter. *Mary Lincoln: Biography of a Marriage.* Little, Brown. 1953.

Reagan, Nancy, with William Novak. *My Turn.* Random House. 1989.

Robbins, Jhan. *Bess & Harry.* G. P. Putnam's Sons. New York. 1980.

Roosevelt, Eleanor. *Eleanor Roosevelt's My Day: Her Acclaimed Columns 1936–1945,* ed. by Rochelle Chadakoff. Pharos. 1989.

———. *Eleanor Roosevelt's My Day: Vol. II: Her Acclaimed Columns 1945–1952,* ed. by David Emblidge. Pharos. 1990.

———. *Eleanor Roosevelt's My Day: Vol. III: Her Acclaimed Columns 1953–1962,* ed. by David Emblidge. Pharos. 1991.

———. *On My Own.* Harper. 1958.

———. *This I Remember.* Harper. 1949.

———. *This Is My Story.* Harper. 1937.

Roosevelt, Theodore. *The Autobiography of Theodore Roosevelt.* Charles Scribner's Sons. 1958.

———. *Theodore Roosevelt's Letters to His Children,* ed. by Joseph Bucklin Bishop. Charles Scribner's Sons. 1931.

Ross, Ishbel. *Grace Coolidge and Her Era.* Dodd, Mead. 1962.

Russell, Francis. *The Shadow of Blooming Grove: Warren Harding in His Times.* McGraw-Hill. 1968.

Saunders, Frances Wright. *Ellen Axson Wilson: First Lady Between Two Worlds.* University of North Carolina Press. 1985.

Sievers, Harry J. *Benjamin Harrison: Hoosier Warrior.* University Publishers. 1952.

———. *Benjamin Harrison: Hoosier Statesman.* University Publishers. 1959.

———. *Benjamin Harrison: Hoosier President.* Bobbs-Merrill. 1968.

Smith, Page. *John Adams: Vol. I: 1735–1784.* Doubleday. 1962.

———. *John Adams: Vol. II: 1784–1826.* Doubleday. 1962.

Smith, Richard Norton. *An Uncommon Man: The Triumph of Herbert Hoover.* Simon and Schuster. 1984.

Thane, Elswyth. *Washington's Lady: The Life of Martha Washington.* Dodd, Mead. 1960.

Thompson, Charles Willis. *Presidents I Have Known and Two Near Presidents.* NP. 1929.

Trefousse, Hans L. *Andrew Johnson: A Biography.* W. W. Norton. 1989.

Truman, Margaret. *Bess W. Truman.* Jove Books. 1986.

———. *First Ladies.* Random House. 1995.

———. *Harry S. Truman.* Morrow. 1972.

Van Der Heuvel, Gerry. *Crowns of Thorns and Glory.* Dutton. 1988.

Whitton, Mary Ormsbee. *First First Ladies 1789–1865: A Study of the Wives of the Early Presidents.* Hastings House. 1948.

Wilson, Edith Bolling. *My Memoir.* Bobbs-Merrill. 1939.

Withey, Lynne. *Dearest Friend: A Life of Abigail Adams.* Free Press. 1981.

Woodward, W. E. *Meet General Grant.* Garden City. 1928.

Index

Martha Washington
1731 - 1802
Abigail Adams
1744-1818
Martha Jefferson
1748-1782
Dolley Madison
1768-1849
Elizabeth Monroe
1768 - 1830
Louisa Adams
1775 - 1852
Rachel Jackson
1767 - 1828
Hannah Van Buren
1783 - 1819
Anna Harrison
1775 - 1864
Letitia Tyler
1790 - 1842
Julia Tyler
1820 - 1889
Sarah Polk
1803 - 1891
Margaret Taylor
1788 - 1852
Abilgail Fillmore
1798 - 1853
Jane Pierce
1806 - 1863
Harriet Lane
1830 - 1903
Mary Lincoln
1818 - 1882
Eliza Johnson
1810 - 1876
Julia Grant
1826 - 1902
Lucy Hayes
1831 - 1889
Lucretia Garfield
1832 - 1918
Ellen Arthur
1837 - 1880